Comfort Quilts
FROM THE Heart

Jake Finch

12 QUICK PROJECTS TO TAKE CARE OF OTHERS

C&T PUBLISHING

Text copyright © 2008 by Jacqueline Finch

Artwork copyright © 2008 by C&T Publishing, Inc.

Publisher: Amy Marson

Editorial Director: Gailen Runge

Acquisitions Editor: Jan Grigsby

Editor: Stacy Chamness

Technical Editors: Helen Frost and Marjorie Russell

Copyeditor: Alix North

Proofreader: Wordfirm Inc.

Design Director/Cover & Book Designer: Christina D. Jarumay

Production Coordinators: Tim Manibusan and Matt Allen

Illustrator: Richard Sheppard

Photography by Luke Mulks and Diane Pedersen of C&T Publishing, unless otherwise noted.

A special thanks to Grangewood Antiques for the use of the rocking chair.
1256 Diamond Way, Concord, CA 94520
www.grangewoodantiques.com

Published by C&T Publishing, Inc., P.O. Box 1456, Lafayette, CA 94549.

Library of Congress Cataloging-in-Publication Data

Finch, Jake,

    Comfort quilts from the heart : 12 quick projects to take care of others / Jake Finch.

        p. cm.

    Summary: "From NICU quilts for babies to quilts for breast cancer patients to sensory-stimulation quilts designed for Alzheimer's patients—within the pages of this book, you will find comfort in creating for someone in need. The designs work up quickly and are well suited for group efforts as well as individual creations" —Provided by publisher.

    ISBN 978-1-57120-492-9 (paper trade : alk. paper)

    1. Patchwork--Patterns. 2. Quilting--Patterns. 3. Patchwork quilts. I. Title.

    TT835.F5416 2008

    746.46'041--dc22

                                    2007044174

Printed in China

10 9 8 7 6 5 4 3 2 1

DEDICATION

This book would not have been possible without the inspiration of those strong people around me, those who have survived terrible illnesses, and those who were taken by them. To my Nana, who left this world before she wanted to because of uterine cancer; to my Grandma, who didn't know her breast cancer had metastasized when she went home; to my stepmother, Gloria, who sits imprisoned by Alzheimer's disease; and to our precious Aubrey, who, even though her light shines now in a mansion with many rooms, will always stay young and bright in the hearts of her family.

ACKNOWLEDGMENTS

My gratitude is always given to the people at C&T Publishing who helped make this book, and my last one, both things I treasure. To my editor, Stacy Chamness, who always, always has a smile in her voice, encouragement in her words, and laughter to share; to Helen Frost who worked so hard with me; to Kiera Lofgreen, for keeping Stacy and me together; to Luke Mulks, Diane Pedersen, Cynthia Bix, Christina Jarumay, and Kristy Zacharias for their wonderful visuals; to Mari Dreyer, Janet Levin, Danielle Dews, and the rest of C&T's marketing team who continue to get the word out; to Jan Grigsby, Gailen Runge, and Amy Marson for always treating me with respect and kindness; and to their delightful office mom, Barbara Sandoval, who makes me and my kid feel so welcome and special when we visit, I thank you all.

To my friends I've mentioned before, and to those who have taken me in since Fast, Fun & Easy Book Cover Art, thank you again for your love and care. The list is so long and the wonderful people on it have never strayed from my side. To my past list, I'd like to add Ryka George; Vince and Ceja Jeffries; Nancy Marie Mauger; Janice Poulus; my sisters, Ronni Herb, Robin Lipner, and Malissa Fine; and my brothers, Peter Fine, Michael Fine, and John Herb.

I want to especially thank the many women and handful of men in the Simi Valley Quilt Guild, the Conejo Valley Quilt Guild, Cotton & Chocolate Quilt Company, Kingdom Sewing & Vacuum, The Quilter's Studio, Quilt Ventura, Quilter's Country Cottage, Baron's Fabrics, and the other regular quilting haunts through whose halls I wander. Without your support, encouragement, expertise, wonderful fabrics, and fantastic inspiration, this would not be a book.

I have also been extremely blessed to meet many professional quilters, and others in related industries, who have willingly offered their wisdom. To Chris Brown and Mark Lipinski, who keep letting me write for them; to Paula Reid, Sharyn Craig, Joan Shay, and Kelly Gallagher-Abbott, who I consider mentors in the finest sense; to the people at Janome who make amazing sewing machines and let me use them; to the finest art quilters found on the Studio Art Quilt Associates and QuiltArt boards, who have freely shared their expertise and awe; and to Lois Hallock, my first and best official quilt buddy, who walks through this crazy combination of young children and shifting careers with me, thank you.

Lastly, to the health professionals who have helped me with their experiences and knowledge to make the information as accurate as possible and the projects as relevant as can be, I so appreciate your efforts in caring for all of our loved ones who are in need.

Table of Contents

Introduction

Comfort Quilts From the Heart was born from my pain in the wake of a great family tragedy. In December 2002, my 18-year-old cousin, Aubrey Lynn Hoskinson, was diagnosed with alveolar rhabdomyosarcoma, a rare and advanced form of pediatric cancer that attacks the soft tissues of infants and older teens. Aubrey and I were very close. For many years, she and her sister, Lydia, were the daughters I longed for, and the suddenness and severity of her illness devastated my family and me.

In my fear and grief, the only action I could take, as I prepared to travel to Sacramento to spend what would be our last Christmas together, was to make a quilt. I wanted something to cheer and inspire Aubrey as she walked her long road of surgery, radiation, and chemotherapy. The quilt had to be bright and happy, but rich and fun to look at. The quilt had to be sized for her new locales—hospital beds and wheelchairs. I wanted it to be warm, and it needed to be finished in two days.

My daughter, Samantha, with Aubrey Lynn Hoskinson, early 2002.

Photo by Jake Finch.

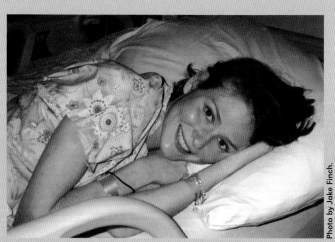

Aubrey during treatment.

Photo by Jake Finch.

I scoured my quilt books for a simple pattern to fit my needs. Nothing was right. I had already picked my two fabrics—a fuchsia batik and violet batik, to use in the quilt. So, I quickly drafted a pattern based on a rail fence block, and set to work.

For two days, my husband took care of our daughter, Samantha, who was a toddler then, while I worked nonstop to finish Aubrey's quilt. On the plane up to Sacramento, I tacked the binding. Before we went to the hospital to see Aubrey, I stitched her label to the back, which I had handwritten on a piece of white fabric. And it was done.

Creating that quilt was cathartic for me. And it must have been for someone else. A couple of days after we left Sacramento, Aubrey was on her way down to surgery, and she brought her quilt. It was placed underneath her gurney. After the surgery, the quilt disappeared. It never made it back upstairs to Aubrey's room.

When my family called me to tell me about the quilt's loss, I was not upset. I still had some of the fabric left, so I told them not to worry, that when I came to see Aubrey in a couple of weeks, I would bring another. This time it would be better, because I had more time to work on it.

Once again, I hit my sewing room and put together another quilt similar to the first. Because I had strip-pieced the first one, I had some strip sets left over to use in the new one. Two weeks later, the new quilt traveled with Samantha and me back to Sacramento, complete with a new label.

Nothing will ever heal me from the pain of losing Aubrey a short seven months later, but I will always treasure the look on her face when she placed the first quilt, and later its sister version, over her damaged body. Each quilt went with her to treatments, and the second followed her home when her time came. The labels on the backs of both quilts were deeply personal, with my words of encouragement and love

Aubrey's first quilt. The photo isn't great, but it's the only surviving proof of the quilt.

and some favorite Bible verses about strength and faith that I hoped would reassure and comfort her when I couldn't be there.

These quilts made me think about all the other quilts I've made or heard of being made for people who were ill. There were the neonatal intensive care unit (NICU) quilts made by members of my guild, the Simi Valley Quilt Guild, for babies in hospitals; the quilts for our guild members fighting breast cancer; and the sensory stimulation quilts I designed for Alzheimer's patients so they would find quilted comfort in a different way—through touch.

My hope is that within the pages of this book, you, too, will find comfort in creating for someone in need. Most of the designs work up quickly and are well suited for group efforts as well as individual creations.

Whether the project is for someone you know or for total strangers who will never meet the maker of the quilt they will hold, all quilts made and given with love can help heal.

Materials, Tools & Techniques

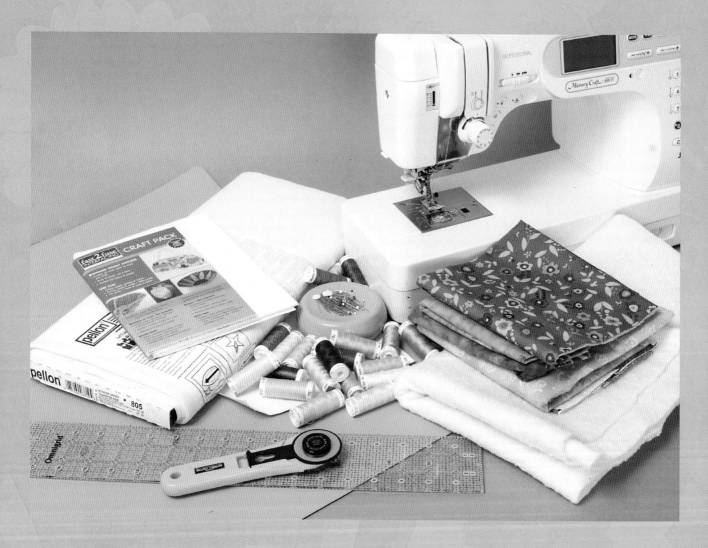

Following are the tools and techniques that work best for me. If you have products you prefer or ways of doing things better suited to your style and skills, go for it. I always advocate doing what works best for you. Some of my methods stray from orthodox quilting techniques, but keep in mind that I designed these projects to be completed quickly, so I have thrown in many of my favorite quilting shortcuts.

Materials

Fabric Choices & Prewashing

When it comes to most of the quilts and projects in this book, I have used good-quality, 100% quilter's cotton. It's the softest cotton I know, is made for the tasks at hand, and, most important, comes in a variety of prints and colors to suit any recipient. In quilting, I firmly believe that you get what you pay for.

The amounts for cotton quilting fabrics used in the projects are based on a 42″ width. Many of the projects use fat quarter and fat eighth cuts of fabric.

> **tip**
> A fat quarter is a piece of quilt fabric, usually cotton, that is approximately 18″ × 22″ (give or take an inch for actual selvage-to-selvage width of the precut fabric).

Fat quarters are easily located at quilt stores and shows, and I consider them tempting eye candy for any quilter! The easiest way to use fats is to look for the prepackaged bundles of coordinating fabrics to work into a project. A perfect example of a fat quarter bundle project is the *Bed Shawl* (page 37). A package of eight coordinated fats will create a beautiful and quick gift for someone spending too much time in bed.

Prepackaged fat quarters make a wonderful starting point for many of the comfort quilts in this book!

> **tip**
> A fat eighth is a piece of quilt fabric approximately 9″ × 22″, give or take an inch.

Fat eighths might be more difficult to find, but they are easily used in some of the projects. The *Concentration Game Quilt* (page 46) was made using fat eighths of children's novelty prints and would work well for an adult by using floral or Asian prints.

There are projects in the book, such as the *Fidget Quilt* (page 19), that use decorator fabrics. These fabrics are more expensive than standard quilter's cottons, but you are not buying much, and they can often be located on discount tables and during store sales. Remember also that decorator fabrics generally come in 54″ widths. That extra 10″ can sometimes make the difference in having enough fabric for a quilt.

Decorator prints are easily found in fabric stores and come in many different types of textures and prints.

You can also combine beautiful printed cottons with fancies, such as velvets and silks, to maintain the tactility of the quilt, while stretching your options and wallet. If you choose to do this, I would still use the ½″ seam allowance recommended in the *Fidget Quilt* project, as it allows the fancies and decorator fabrics to comfortably settle with their less-raveling neighbors, the tightly woven cottons. Fuse a very lightweight interfacing to the back of quilter's cottons or other lightweight fabrics to help "match" the weights of the fabrics. This allows your finished quilt to wear more evenly by strengthening the lighter-weight fabrics.

Because all of these quilts are destined to become gifts for people who are ill, *please be sure to prewash the fabrics*. This has nothing to do with my personal opinion on one of the greatest quilting debates around—to wash or not to wash. There is a practical, considerate reason for prewashing fabrics for these types of quilts. People undergoing radiation, chemotherapy, and other treatments that suppress a person's immune system will be extra sensitive to the chemicals used to treat fabrics.

Use a gentle, allergen- and fragrance-free detergent to prepare your fabrics and to wash the final product. The washing should happen both before putting the projects together and then after the project is finished, so any oils and chemicals on your hands or workspace are completely removed from your work.

When I prewash decorator fabrics, I place the whole piece in a lingerie bag for both the washing and drying of the fabrics on the gentle cycles. If the fabric won't hold up to the washing, it shouldn't be used. Assuming it does hold up, and most will, it will need to be trimmed of any raw threads along the cut edges. After trimming, carefully iron. Watch your iron's temperature. Many of these fabrics will be made from synthetic fibers, and you don't want to burn or melt them.

Interfacing

For one of the projects in the book, the *Walker Bag* (page 51), I turned to the materials and techniques I discovered and developed while creating my book cover projects for *Fast, Fun & Easy Book Cover Art* (C&T Publishing, 2007).

The interfacing I use is fast2fuse—a double-sided fusible interfacing that comes in two weights, regular and heavy, and is available in most quilt shops. At 28″ wide, it's also the widest heavy interfacing on the market. Another type of heavy interfacing is Timtex, which does not have a fusible coating on the material. To use Timtex, you must purchase enough lightweight fusible web, such as Steam-A-Seam 2, to join the fabric to both sides of the interfacing. Both brands of heavy interfacings are washable and lend themselves to many craft projects.

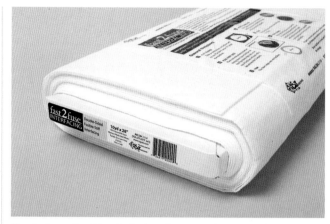

Hands down, fast2fuse is the best heavyweight interfacing currently on the market.

When combining photo transfer fabrics or quilter's cottons with decorator prints, such as in the *Fidget Quilt*, I use a lightweight fusible interfacing ironed onto the back of the transfers or cottons. This helps to match the weights of the fabrics, which offsets the overall wear of the finished quilt. When you have blocks with such differing weights next to each other, the heavier weighted fabrics will stretch and pull too much on their lighter weight neighbors. Follow the manufacturer's instructions completely when fusing the interfacing.

Basting Spray

Years ago, I was on the brink of making the drastic decision to stop quilting because I hated basting quilts! It didn't matter if I used pins, tacks, or thread. It was the worst part of quiltmaking for me. And then some heavenly Fabric Angel developed spray baste, and my quilting was rescued from the depths of my despair.

To this day, I swear by 505 Spray and Fix temporary spray adhesive for basting quilts or holding appliqué pieces in place. Yes, there are other brands on the market, but I've had the best experiences with 505 by far. With it, there is almost no gummy residue left on my needles. It is stainless, odorless, and acid free. Follow the manufacturer's instructions carefully. Remember to wash your final project to avoid exposing sensitive patients to the chemicals.

When you are making a project that uses microfleece (such as Minkee) for a backing, use spray baste to bond the layers before quilting. Microfleeces, when left alone to layer with cotton or other fabric, will shift, move, and wiggle like a GI swing dancing in the 1940s. The only solution I've found to completely tame the flighty nature of microfleece is to spray baste it with authority. Only then will your fleece obey your commands.

Fusible Web

When choosing a fusible web, select a lightweight, permanent product. You'll be using the fusible to bond fabric to fabric for appliqué and, if using a nonfusible interfacing, to bond fabric to the interfacing. With all the other layers in your quilt, you want the least amount of added bulk possible for smooth sewing. My favorite is Steam-A-Seam 2. It comes in large rolls and allows for repositioning of your fabric before you permanently bond it with an iron.

Thread

For piecing, I use good-quality cotton thread in a neutral color. My current favorite thread is Aurifil. It is a long-staple spun cotton thread used for machine quilting, so there's much less shedding (which causes lint buildup in your machine) than other brands I've found.

Threads are an important part of any quilting project.

As for quilting, and I free-motion quilt all of my quilts on my home sewing machine, I admit I never used to pay much attention to thread. At quilt shows, I noticed when a pretty metallic thread jazzed up a quilt, but I never thought to use it in my work. Honestly, the thought of getting unusual threads to obey my commands left me intimidated. No longer is this my reality! I love thread. I love the effects it offers to an otherwise simple piece of fabric or quilt block. The trick with using any thread beyond your standard cotton is to know with what needle it works best. Ask your store owner, look it up in a book on machine quilting and thread use, or look it up on the manufacturer's website. Oftentimes, the thread used can

enhance simple quilting. Experiment when those beautiful, shiny threads call to you from their racks.

> **tip**
>
> *I use Robison-Anton's rayon thread for my edgestitching (see the Walker Bag, page 51). The threads work well in my machine, offer an elegant finish, and are sturdier in my experience than other types of rayon thread. When selecting the color, choose a complementary solid to the fabric for both the top and bobbin threads. It's the most forgiving option if your machine's tension is off just a little, and offers the cleanest edge possible. (Literally! It also repels dirt better than cotton thread.)*

Batting

For the projects in this book, batting is a rich subject. Your ultimate goal for all of these projects is comfort, and that sometimes means using nontraditional batting or leaving it out of your finished project altogether.

I used one of three batting choices in the projects: thin cotton batting, flannel, or no batting.

Warm & Natural is my personal favorite because I free-motion quilt on my machine. It's thin enough to allow for easy needle action, and it doesn't have to be prewashed. Always wash the finished project to clean the batting and other materials that aren't prewashed.

I use flannel when I want a heavier hand in the finished quilt. It's still a soft option for the quilt, but in the case of the *Bed Shawl* (page 37) and *Fidget Quilt* (page 19), having flannel between the layers offered body to the quilts. Prewash flannel before using it, as it has a high shrinkage potential.

There are also some projects where I have simply used microfleece fabrics on the back. The fleece gave more than enough body to the project and also offered the depth needed for simple machine quilting.

When I do use batting with microfleece, I have discovered that Warm & Natural is my best choice because fleeces are knits. The dense, all-cotton, needle-punched batting, when spray basted to the fleece's back, acts as a stabilizer for the knit's stretch factor.

tip

Before making final choices on whether or not to batt, prepare a 10˝ sample square for each option, and quilt it quickly to get a feel for the project's final hand. Keep these samples to refer back to when deciding how to complete a project.

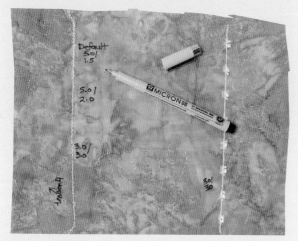

Keep your quilted samples handy for reference when planning your next project.

Photo Transfer Papers & Fabrics

The craft market these days is overflowing with materials designed to merge photos with fabric surfaces. You can print photographs—either scanned into your computer or downloaded from discs or the Internet—onto special iron transfer paper in your printer. There are fabrics specially treated and sized to run through your printer to print a photo directly onto the fabric. There are even chemicals available that enable you to make your own printer-sized photo fabric sheets.

There are many different types of photo transfer supplies to incorporate memories in your comfort projects.

I will quickly say that I have had the best success working with the Printed Treasures fabric sheets by Milliken. Found in craft stores, these sheets run through the printer easily, take color beautifully, and don't require any special handling, like heat setting or rinsing, to work. They are pricey, so carefully test your print before using the sheets in your printer. But for color and durability, they are great.

You will also need access to a simple photo-editing program. Look for computer programs that crop, resize, and allow you to play with the photo's colors. I use Adobe Elements (see Sources, page 78).

Fuse a lightweight fusible interfacing to the back of the photo transfers to use with decorator prints, such as in the *Fidget Quilt* (page 19). This helps to match the weights of the fabrics.

It is essential that you follow the manufacturer's instructions completely when using your transfer mediums, whether paper or fabric.

Tools

Rotary Cutters, Mats & Rulers

You'll need at least a medium 45mm rotary cutter, with extra blades for the projects. I use a large 60mm cutter; it allows me to cut many layers at once, saving lots of time and wrist wear. I prefer the rotary cutters that have a safety button and retractable blade, as cutters are truly dangerous tools when not watched. In my classes, I usually have my students memorize my favorite quilting mantra, "Never turn your back on your rotary cutter." Because I work with both fabric and paper regularly, I have dedicated one rotary cutter to only paper and one to fabric. To cut fast2fuse, I use the paper blade because it doesn't need to be as sharp as when cutting fabric. Most quilters have two pairs of scissors as well.

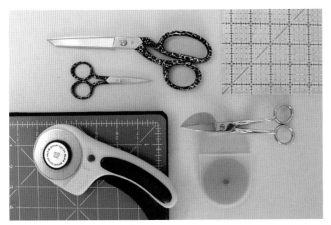
Cutting tools are an important investment for any quilter.

Rotary cutter mats are self-healing, printed with a 1″ grid, and have marks at ⅛″ intervals. It is a wonderful tool to include in your arsenal of creative implements. A mat that's at least 18″ × 24″ should take you through most projects, though the larger mats are much easier to use if you have the surface area.

Quilter's rulers come in a huge assortment of sizes and colors. In general, they are made from clear Lucite and are marked with grid lines spaced at least a ¼″ apart. You will need at least two to comfortably make most of the projects. Use a 6″ × 24″ or 8½″ × 24″ as your main ruler, and a square ruler at least 12″ (even bigger is better) as a backup ruler.

There is another type of ruler that I use for paper piecing that is a wonderful extra tool. It's called an Add-A-Quarter by CM Designs (see Sources, page 78) and widely available at quilt shops and online resources. This ruler has a ¼″ lip along its edge that hugs the folded paper and allows for easier trimming while paper piecing. You can live without it, but it's a small investment for a big difference in paper piecing. I recommend the 12″ size, as the 6″ size is limiting.

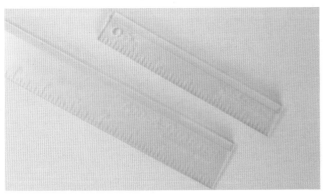
Add-A-Quarter rulers make all the difference in paper piecing.

One of the techniques listed in the instructions for some of the projects is "fussy cutting." Fussy cutting is when you position your cutting to take advantage of a specific area of the fabric, usually to center a motif.

Iron & Accessories

There are several great debates among quilters that will never be resolved, and what kind of iron to use is one of them. Use what you prefer, ignoring all the voices out there. Read the fusible manufacturer's directions thoroughly when you're ironing your fusible products, as some use steam and others don't.

Sewing Machine & Accessories

Sewing machines can be as unique as the person who operates them, which makes it very hard to say which ones will work the best for you. The quilted projects will work well with most machines, and, for these efforts, a ¼″ foot is your best friend, the exception being the *Fidget Quilt*, which uses ½″ seam allowances. You can also use a piece of masking tape to mark a scant ¼″ or ½″ on your sewing machine bed to use as a guide for feeding your fabric. A scant ¼″ is about one thread less than a true ¼″. It's a common quilting reference because the scant part allows for the pressing of the seams to result in a true ¼″ finished seam.

If you're going to quilt your own finished tops, and I urge you to try, you will need a darning foot, sometimes called a free-motion foot. It allows you to see the surface of the quilt as you quilt. It also rests on top of the quilt but allows for the free movement of the quilt underneath.

Another very helpful attachment is an even-feed foot, sometimes called a walking foot. This attachment helps move the layers of fabric through the machine's feed dogs at the same pace. It's especially helpful with the decorator fabrics and microfleeces.

For the *Walker Bag* project (page 51), your machine needs to be able to create a tight satin stitch and to sew through bulky, heavyweight fabrics. Most modern machines will take care of these tasks with the proper needle and thread.

In case you're curious, and many students regularly ask this of me, I use Janome sewing machines. I've owned other brands, but Janomes are my machine of choice. In the end, use what works best for your skills, preferences, and wallet.

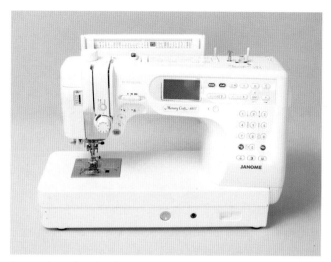

Janome is my favorite, but use what works for you.

Needles

Sewing machine needles are probably the most important tools in your notions case. Because your machine is going to be working very hard punching through different layers and weights of materials, your needles will either enable or inhibit you from the start. I have had the best and most consistent luck with Schmetz brand needles. For piecing standard cotton fabrics, I use Schmetz sharps, usually 80/12 or 90/14 for heavier fabrics. For really heavy decorator prints, I sometimes turn to a denim/jeans needle, but I always try with the larger sharps needles first. For the quilting and edgestitching on fast2fuse, I use Schmetz topstitch needles. These needles are sturdier and their eyes are designed to allow for the easy flow of many types of decorative threads.

All of my projects were finished with either an 80/12 topstitch or 90/14 topstitch needle. I use one needle for each project and willingly change to a new needle at the first sign of trouble. If you pay attention, you can hear your needle working harder as it wears out. If your thread starts breaking or your stitching progress seems sluggish, change your needle.

Quilter's Gloves

Any type of machine quilting is helped along immensely when you wear quilter's gloves. They provide traction against the fabric and are almost mandatory when aiming for happy free-motion quilting. An inexpensive, but warm, alternative is medical gloves, without powder. The lightweight rubber also provides adequate traction.

If you are more comfortable using paddles or silicon sprays on the bed of your machine, stick with it. In the end, I always say to use what works best for you.

Quiltmaking Techniques

As I so readily admit, I am a self-taught quilter. Learning from many of the wonderful primers on quiltmaking over the years, I was already teaching to beginners when I took my first class. That means that I have managed to (A) make every quilt mistake known to quiltkind, and (B) learn various shortcuts that go against the grain (sorry for the pun) of traditional quiltmaking. Some of my favorite shortcuts are used for borders and bindings. While I have learned to do it the right way over the last few years, I have reverted to some of my shortcuts in this book because they are the fastest method for me to make a quilt. To me, you can't make comfort quickly enough. If I offer anything in these techniques that you don't want to try, don't. If you're a member of the quilt police, don't report me. Just turn to your tried-and-true methods and get the project done.

Cutting

Most of the projects use strips that are cut selvage to selvage across the fabric. Any pieces cut lengthwise are noted in the project cutting instructions.

An easy and efficient way to cut fat quarters into strips is to first stack them. Iron, then stack up to six fat quarters at a time, lining up the selvage edge and one long edge. Trim one edge, either the selvage or the long edge as noted in the project directions. Then cut strips, beginning at the trimmed edge.

Stacking and trimming fat quarters saves lots of time.

Seam Allowances

A scant $\frac{1}{4}$″ seam allowance is used for most projects. It's a good idea to do a test seam before you begin sewing to check the accuracy of your $\frac{1}{4}$″ seam. When working with decorator fabrics and anything else that is heavy-weight, I use $\frac{1}{2}$″ seam allowances. This enables me to have plenty of fabric for pressing seams open, another shift from traditional quilting. Because decorator fabrics are heavy and prone to shredding at the cut edges, having a larger seam allowance gives your seams added security.

Pressing

In general, press seams toward the darker fabric. Press firmly and slowly in an up-and-down motion. Make sure your seams are completely flat (no small amounts of fabric still folded into them); you don't want to over-iron, which can distort shapes and blocks. When using decorator fabrics—as you will be doing with some of the *fidget quilts* (page 19)—press your seams open instead of to one side. This distributes the bulk from the heavier fabric and helps with the final quilting. Set your iron to the appropriate heat—many decorator fabrics are made from synthetics that easily burn or melt.

Machine Appliqué Using Fusible Adhesive

1. Place the fusible web paper-side up on the pattern and trace with a thin permanent marker. Trace detail lines with a permanent marker for ease in transferring to the fabric.

2. Use paper-cutting scissors to roughly cut out the pieces. Leave at least a $\frac{1}{4}$″ margin.

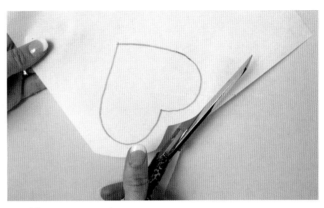

Roughly cut out your pieces.

3. Following the manufacturer's instructions, fuse the web pattern to the wrong side of the appliqué fabric. It helps to use an appliqué-pressing sheet to avoid getting the adhesive on your iron or ironing board.

4. Cut out pieces along the outside lines. Do not remove the paper yet.

Trim the appliqué piece to the line.

5. Transfer detail lines (if any) to the fabric by placing the piece on a light table or up to the window and marking the fabric. Use a chalk pencil for this task—the lines will be covered by thread.

6. Remove the paper and position the appliqué piece on the project. Be sure the web (rough) side is down. Press in place, following the manufacturer's instructions.

7. Finish the appliqué by sewing along the inside edge of the appliqué piece. You can use a decorative stitch such as a blanket stitch or a straight stitch. The goal is to get some stitching to secure the appliqué piece down because with repeated washing, the fusible bond will lift over time.

tip *Have fun with all the decorative stitching on your appliqué pieces.*

Borders

WARNING

Here is one of those unorthodox quilt moments. Remember, if you have a better way to do what needs to be done, ignore me and do it!

For most of the projects with borders, cut the strips from selvage to selvage. Piece the strips together to make longer pieces if necessary. If a border strip is more than 3″ wide, piece all of the strips together with a straight seam and press the seam open. When working with strips that are less than 3″ wide, piece them at right angles and press the seams open to provide more stability for working with the strips. You're ready now to attach the borders.

Starting on one of the longest sides, pin the border strip to the quilt, leaving 2″–3″ extra at the end. Trim the other end, again leaving 2″–3″ extra. Repeat the process for the opposite side.

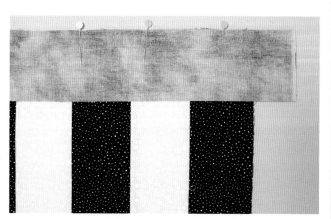

Pin border strip to quilt, leaving about 3″ extra on either end.

Using a ¼″ seam allowance, sew each border to the quilt. Press the seams to the darker fabric and then use a large square ruler or an 8½″ × 24″ ruler to trim the corners square. Repeat the same steps for the other sides of the quilt. While I have been told this method could create borders that cause the quilt not to lie flat, I have not had this happen yet.

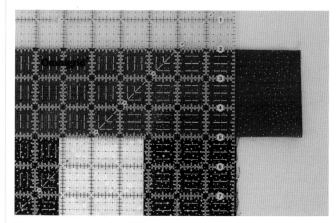

Your square rotary ruler will become one of your better quilting friends.

Sandwiching & Basting

Cut or piece the backing to make it a minimum of 2″ larger than the quilt top on all sides. Prewash the fabric and trim the selvages before you piece, using a ¼″ seam allowance. To economize, you can piece the back from any leftover fabrics or blocks in your collection. Press your backing well and fold it neatly until you're ready to sandwich your quilt.

I so strongly recommend spray basting that I haven't provided guidance for pin or hand basting. Sorry, but those are techniques you can easily find in other places. Instead, I swear by 505 Spray and Fix. A small can will usually baste up to a queen-sized quilt.

The benefits from spray basting include:

■ Much less time is needed to baste your projects.

■ There is an even dispersal of adhesive throughout your layers, which enables you to quilt better with less puckering. This is especially important when basting any project using microfleece or other unorthodox fabrics on the back.

When spray basting, use either large tables put together (many quilt shops let customers use their tables for this purpose, but be sure they know it's for spray basting) or a clean floor. I use the carpet in my sewing studio. Whether on tables or floor:

1. Position the backing, wrong side up, on the floor, making sure the backing is very smooth.

2. Lay the batting on top, making sure it's centered on the backing layer. Smooth the batting over the backing.

3. Fold back the batting halfway onto itself and spray baste by quickly and evenly spraying across the exposed wrong side of the backing and the batting. (This contradicts the manufacturer's instructions, but I've found spraying both layers works best.)

4. Slowly unfold the batting back onto the backing, using large, even sweeps of your hand to smooth the bat-ting onto the backing from the center out. (If the quilt is large, this may take another pair of hands to accomplish. One person holds the batting over the backing as the other smoothes the layers together slowly.)

5. When the 2 layers are adhered together, repeat the process on the other half of the backing/batting layers.

6. Without lifting the backing/batting layers, lay the quilt top on the batting, making sure the top is well pressed. Repeat the spray process—folding the top back halfway, spraying both exposed layers, then smoothing the layers back together.

7. For larger quilts or if needed, press the basted sandwich outward from the center to ensure there are no small puckers.

Spray quickly and evenly over both exposed layers.

Smooth the layers together.

■ Spray baste is repositionable, so if you have a really ugly crease or pucker, gently lift the layers apart and re-smooth into place.

■ It almost always holds until the project is washed, even if you can't get around to the quilting for several weeks. If there's any shifting, the adhesive can be reactivated by pressing a steam iron over the project.

Quilting

As the purpose of these projects is to get them done quickly, and as some of the fabrics are microfleece, decorator fabrics, and other uncommon quilt materials, you will be better off machine quilting. Don't be afraid of machine quilting. It can be as simple as quilting-in-the-ditch or using some other straight-line patterns. If you're comfortable with machine quilting, free-motion patterns will get you finished the quickest. Practice on your sample sandwich first when working with materials you're not used to, such as the decorator fabrics or microfleece.

To free-motion quilt, drop the feed dogs on your machine and attach a darning foot or quilting foot, usually provided with the machine. The darning foot rests on top of the quilt top but moves up and down with the needle, enabling the quilt to move freely underneath the foot. When you become proficient with machine quilting, you should find that it's almost as simple as pencil drawing, where a line appears where you place the instrument.

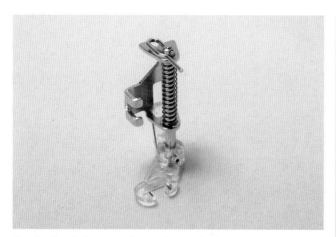
Darning feet look strange but work great for free-motion quilting.

I've learned a couple of tricks over the years that work well for me on my machine. They might also help you succeed in machine quilting. I use a single-needle plate on my machine's bed. This prevents the fabric from being pushed into the machine's bobbin casing as I'm quilting, especially at high speeds. For my needle, I use a Schmetz topstitch in 80/12 size, unless the fabric is heavy and then I use a 90/14 size. For me, topstitch needles work best because I usually quilt with rayon threads on the top, and the rayon moves more smoothly through this kind of needle.

One of the most important things I've learned for machine quilting is to use Libby Lehman's *The Bottom Line* threads by Superior Threads in my bobbin. This thread has been a quilt-saver for me! It's a super-thin, super-strong spun polyester thread that leaves almost no lint. Because it's so thin, I can fill my bobbins with almost twice as much thread, which means fewer interruptions to re-bobbin my machine. And, because it's so thin, it moves through my bobbin happier than any other thread I've worked with. It comes in a full rainbow of colors, but I stock up on the neutrals and that carries me through most quilting projects.

This combination of needle/thread/plate has allowed my free-motion quilting to take off over the last few years. But every machine and every user is different, so experiment to find the best combination of tools and techniques in your machine quilting.

As far as quilting patterns, I'm usually so rushed for time that I decide upon a stippling pattern and run with that. As a result, I've become very adept at stippling. Stippling is simply an all-over meandering pattern where your thread lines avoid crossing. It could be curls, waves, stars, hearts, spirals, or anything else that covers the ground of your quilt top. There are several excellent books on the market to learn machine-quilting techniques.

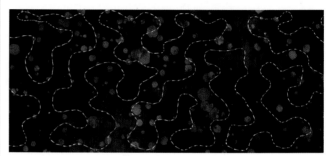
Stippling is an all-over pattern that fills space. Ideally, your quilting lines shouldn't cross over each other inadvertently.

When I'm finished quilting, I press my quilt thoroughly and then trim the batting/backing edges to the quilt top's edges using my large square rotary ruler or 8½″ × 24″ ruler. Using the ruler's markings as a guide along the *sewn seam of the closest border*, I trim to whatever width I want the finished border to be, making sure to add a ¼″ for my final seam allowance. I also make sure my corners are perfectly square. Sometimes I will even add an extra inch to the borders as I'm cutting them before piecing for the finished size to allow for easier trimming. It's always more accurate to cut down your project to size at its end than to try to get the measurements to be exact when you're finished. Again, while some may say this will cause edge distortion in the quilt, I have never had a quilt wave at me.

Binding

This is another one of these sections where you will want to seek a more definitive quiltmaking tome to do your binding the right way. Because many of the quilt projects in the book use something plush on the back, I often end up sewing my binding down by machine instead of tacking it in place with hand stitching. While hand stitching is my true preference because I can keep my hubby company in front of the television while I do it, it's nearly impossible to try to tack down plush backing, especially when the backing has been spray basted into place.

In general, I prefer a binding that is sewn a ¼˝ from the edge on the quilt's front and about a ½˝ on the quilt's back. I use a double-fold binding, always made from 2½˝-wide selvage-to-selvage strips. I like 2½˝ because it gives me a lot to tack down on the back, and the width is a common strip width used in piecing and other techniques, which means I can often use leftover strips for binding. My personal trick for successful binding is to use my iron liberally. I like creases in my binding. I also like everything to lie flat. That's how my iron, with steam, helps.

1. Piece 2½˝ strips (2⅛˝ if you're with the quilt police) right sides together with a 45° diagonal seam (corner to corner) to make a continuous binding strip. Trim seam allowance to ¼˝ and press seams open. Then press the entire strip in half lengthwise with wrong sides together. Carefully match the raw edges perfectly.

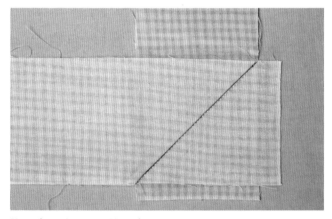

Piece the strips at a 45° angle.

2. With raw edges meeting at the quilt's outside edges, pin the binding to the edge of the quilt a few inches away from a corner. Leave the first few inches of the binding unattached. Start sewing, using a ¼˝ seam allowance. Using an even-feed or walking foot is very helpful for attaching the binding, especially when working with decorator prints and blanket binding as we do with the *Fidget Quilts* (page 19).

Pin the binding to the quilt's edge.

3. Stop sewing ¼˝ away from the first corner and backstitch one stitch. Lift the presser foot and needle. Rotate the quilt a quarter turn. Fold the binding at a right angle so it extends straight above the quilt. Then bring the binding strip down even with the edge of the quilt. Begin sewing at the folded edge, continuing until the next corner. Repeat for each corner.

Miter the binding corners.

4. As you reach the start of the binding, overlap the ends and trim the excess length. Open the binding and fold and press the end.

Fold and press the binding end.

5. Tuck the other end of the binding inside the folded end. Smooth to ensure that there are no tucks or folds in the binding and that it lies perfectly flat to the quilt. Pin well and continue to stitch ¼″ from the edge, finishing a little past the start of your binding.

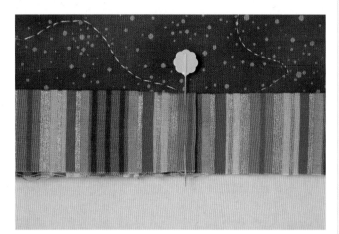

Tuck the end into the binding for a clean finish.

6. With a hot iron, press the binding to the outside edge of the quilt around the whole quilt. At each corner, use the iron's tip to flatten it just a little.

Press the corner well, and you'll have a beautiful mitered corner.

7. Turn the quilt over and carefully press the binding to the back side, making sure to keep the width consistent and the binding completely covering the quilt's edges without leaving "unfilled" areas. At each corner, neatly fold the binding to form a perfect mitered corner. Then pin the binding in place on the back every 6″.

Your iron is your partner in making perfect binding.

8. Using the stitch of your choice, tack the binding in place at the back.

Paper Piecing

One of the projects in this book, the *Wheelchair Quilt* (page 26), uses a simple paper-piecing technique to assemble the blocks. I wrote the directions for the paper piecing specific to those flying geese blocks, so please refer to that chapter for directions.

Mending the Mind:
A Fidget Quilt

42" × 42"

F idget quilts, also called sensory stimulation quilts, are therapeutic quilts used to stimulate people with brain impairments. An obvious recipient is a patient suffering from Alzheimer's disease, the most common of several diseases lumped under the category of dementia.

Alzheimer's is a tragic, degenerative, and fatal brain condition that generally affects people over 65 years old. It has no known cause and no known cure. According to the Alzheimer's Association, 5.1 million Americans were diagnosed with Alzheimer's in 2007. The average life expectancy for an Alzheimer's patient is eight years, but the range spans from three to twenty years. Alzheimer's patients generally begin to lose their short-term memory and other brain functions and, over time, their physical abilities.

Suffice it to say Alzheimer's is a horrible, tragic disease—as are all forms of dementia—that rends not just the patients, but also the caregivers, victims. My stepmother, Gloria Fine, was diagnosed with Alzheimer's about eight years ago but had probably started showing symptoms years before. Medication has slowed the disease's progress, but we know there is no cure. It's hard to describe how deeply this illness affects everyone around the patient. The lifestyle changes required are enormous, and there is no hope for recovery in the patient's day-to-day struggles.

Because patients with Alzheimer's and other dementias experience an ongoing decrease in their brain's functions, simple, repetitive movements and sensory experiences become more important. That's where fidget quilts come in. With their intentional variety of textures and doodads, fidget quilts provide comfort through the hands and the eyes.

Maureen Simons, director of Senior Concerns, a wonderful adult daycare center in Thousand Oaks, California, for Alzheimer's disease victims and patients with dementia, says fidget quilts are calming objects. Area guilds have made fidget quilts for Simons's clients. "It's amazing to watch somebody sit with a quilt held in his or her arms and rock," she says.

Fidget quilts can also benefit anyone suffering from brain trauma and impairments. Accident victims, stroke patients and those with other dementias will find themselves touching more, using their tactility for comfort. The basic premise behind these quilts can even be adapted for children.

Several years ago, my mother had a near-fatal stroke at the age of 57. During her recovery, we discovered one of the areas of her brain that was permanently harmed was her eyesight. Suddenly, her sense of touch became much more important. The texture of things and her ability to discern them became a link to the world around her when her eyesight couldn't provide her the information it had once offered.

Special Features of Fidget Quilts

Fidget quilts have some specific features that can be adapted to the needs of your loved ones:

1. In general, the fabrics used are decorator prints cut into medium-sized squares, about 7″ unfinished/ 6″ finished, which allow the user to enjoy each fabric's distinctive look and feel. Decorator fabrics have their own personality and need to be handled differently from your traditional quilter's cottons. Please refer to *Materials, Tools & Techniques* starting on page 6.

2. There are several buttons, doodads, beads, and/or scrapbook embellishments that are securely attached to the quilt for the user to fondle.

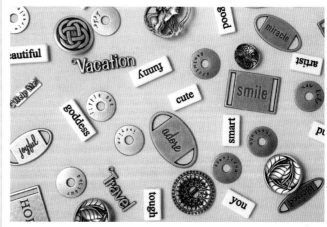

Doodads add stuff to play with on your quilts.

3. Old or sentimental photographs are incorporated into the quilt using photo transfers on specially treated fabric sheets that are run through your printer. These photos offer a memory link and conversation starting point. The photos can be images of people, places, or

things such as cars or houses—anything that once brought or still brings the recipient joy.

Photos of anything special to the recipient can easily be added to your quilt.

4. A list of personal statements about the person that could encourage conversation between a patient and caregiver, especially in a setting like a residential facility or daycare center, or some other type of writing that could sooth the recipient, like a favorite poem, song, or Bible verse. For the *Gentleman's Fidget Quilt* (pictured on page 25), the list of information includes:

- Full name
- Birthplace
- Birth date
- Mother's name
- Father's name
- Occupation
- Spouse and wedding date
- Children and grandchildren
- Favorite hobbies
- Current address

If any of the information seems too personal, leave it out. But it is interesting to offer enough information that a caregiver could try to reach the patient through conversation or even find some common ground upon which to communicate.

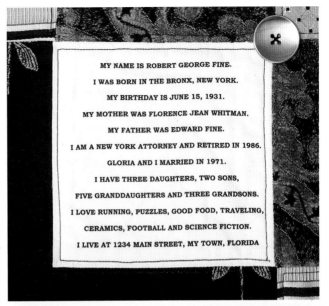

MY NAME IS ROBERT GEORGE FINE.
I WAS BORN IN THE BRONX, NEW YORK.
MY BIRTHDAY IS JUNE 15, 1931.
MY MOTHER WAS FLORENCE JEAN WHITMAN.
MY FATHER WAS EDWARD FINE.
I AM A NEW YORK ATTORNEY AND RETIRED IN 1986.
GLORIA AND I MARRIED IN 1971.
I HAVE THREE DAUGHTERS, TWO SONS,
FIVE GRANDDAUGHTERS AND THREE GRANDSONS.
I LOVE RUNNING, PUZZLES, GOOD FOOD, TRAVELING,
CERAMICS, FOOTBALL AND SCIENCE FICTION.
I LIVE AT 1234 MAIN STREET, MY TOWN, FLORIDA

Using Embellishments on Your Quilt

Patients with dementia and Alzheimer's disease often display behaviors and physical limitations reminiscent of young children. Small objects can become choking hazards to people who retest their world through taste. *Any buttons and doodads used on a fidget quilt must be attached as securely as possible.* If the quilt is intended for someone you know and visit, you might make a point of routinely checking the quilt's doodads to ensure they are not coming loose.

The doodads and buttons I used were purchased in craft and scrapbooking stores, but you could use items that are more personal for your quilt. Jewelry (not valuable, as quilts can be lost or stolen), trinkets, buttons from favorite clothing, old house or car keys, and patches are all things that can be added to your quilt.

Working with Decorator Fabrics

When I'm cutting decorator fabrics, I use a fresh blade in a large rotary cutter. I only cut one layer at a time. No stacking here because when they are stacked, the fabrics can shift easily. Also, if you use fabrics that have raised designs, perhaps with embroidery or additional stitching, try to fussy cut the squares so you aren't piecing over the raised sections. Otherwise, you may need to trim any bulky embellishments or just not use that fabric. Finally, when you're cutting, keep in mind any large design areas and how they will look pieced in the blocks. Again, fussy cutting may be the best way to work with some of those gorgeous patterns!

When I piece decorator fabrics, whether to other heavy fabrics or to lighter weight cottons and silkies, I always use a ½″ seam allowance, and then I press the seams open. This runs contrary to traditional quiltmaking, but we're not working with traditional quilt fabrics. By pressing the seams open, you will have less bulk at your intersections and more room for potential fraying along your raw edges.

Many decorator fabrics are heavily textured. When you're piecing these piled, shiny, or plush fabrics with fabrics that are a little calmer to the touch, you may struggle with shifting and other issues. There are three things that you can do to help alleviate your frustration while sewing:

1. Use a walking foot (sometimes called an even-feed foot) if your machine has one. A walking foot guides both the top and the bottom fabrics under the presser foot at the same pace, offsetting slipping.

2. Pin, pin, pin. Ask anyone who knows me, and they will tell you that in most cases, I'm allergic to pins. But when you're working with fabrics that easily shift, pins become your sewing saviors. On 7″ squares of decorator fabric, I will use 3 to 5 pins. Also, decorator fabrics may

be thicker and denser than cottons, so use long, sharp pins. It will make your job much easier.

3. Starch is a wonderful way to add body to more silky or flimsy fabrics, which, in turn, will help with the piecing. I use regular-weight spray starch bought in the laundry aisle in the supermarket. If you have another option, go for it. Spray a light coating on the fabric and press with the iron. Also, test a scrap beforehand as some silkies may end up with starch stains. Don't use starch on your photo transfers. It will leave spots.

Transferring Memories to Your Quilt

There is some basic information on making photo transfers in *Materials, Tools & Techniques*, on page 10. Please read it before moving ahead as the information there will help make your transfers a success.

With that said, here are some additional points about photo transfers for this project.

1. **When you are selecting pictures for your project, keep in mind your recipient and his or her background.** For instance, if you are making the quilt for someone who is proud of his family, family photos are the best. Those wonderful old photos of generations past can be delightful additions for a fidget quilt, especially if your recipient can easily identify the subjects. Photos of themself as a child can also offer comfort, as can photos of their children when they were young. Long-term memories seem to last the longest for those with brain impairments, and they will be more likely to remember their children as kids. Search for a photo from a family gathering. You can adjust the pattern to make the photo larger, which is very helpful when there are many faces in the picture to identify. Your label on the back of the quilt can even list the people shown in the photo so others can help name who is there.

2. While family photos are natural choices for your fidget quilt, they are not the only choices available. Maybe your recipient has or had a beloved pet? Photos of cats, dogs, horses, or other furry companions (or non-furry for that matter) can be comforting reminders for a loved one. Another option is a favorite home or building. Maybe she loves to reminisce about grandpa's farm, and you're able to track down a photo of the place. Include it. Photos can always be scanned in. Even if you don't have a scanner, you can ask a friend to scan it and copy it onto a disk, or bring it to a copy shop where they will be able to scan your pictures. I can easily see including photos of cherished cars, vacation spots, prize-winning projects (like a quilt?), former schools, favorite artworks, places of business, or anything else that brings on warm memories for your recipient. Maybe he is a fan of a certain movie or musical group? Search the Internet for pictures of movie posters, album covers, publicity photos, or movie stills for images to connect them with their passion.

tip As long as you are using the image for personal use and not selling the finished quilt, you should be fine as far as copyright is concerned.

3. Include some inspirational words. Favorite Bible verses, poems, quotes, proverbs, sayings, or even jokes can be included. Again, the point is to connect your recipient with the quilt on a personal level. Maybe she loved to play a certain classical piece on the piano? Scan in a page of sheet music for the piece and print that onto your photo transfer fabric. Did your recipient take great pride in his college years? Include a scan of their diploma. Maps might also hold special associations for someone. Be creative and considerate, and you will end up with a fidget quilt that provides great joy for someone else.

4. Edit your photos. While re-sizing and cropping your photos, it is also helpful to be able to change the coloring of a photo, even to turn it black and white, as I've done with mine. Because I was working with a mix of old and new photos, I liked the symmetry offered by making all the photos black and white. Many programs will let you change the photo's colors to a sepia brown hue, which would complement warm-colored fabrics nicely. You could even use the special effects available on some photo-editing programs to turn your photos into line drawings, paintings, or graphic prints.

5. Center the photo on the printable fabric. Practice makes perfect. Leave enough area around the photo for a ½″ seam allowance. Transfer papers are expensive. Print a test copy of whatever you're printing on regular paper to check the color and the proportion.

tip Make a paper collage or frame the paper prints to not waste them.

Making the Fidget Quilt

Materials

- ¼ yard each of 4 coordinated decorator fabrics for blocks A, B, C, and D

- ½ yard each of 3 coordinated decorator fabrics for blocks E, F, and G

- 5 photo or word transfers, 7″ × 7″ each

tip Your image needs to be 6″ × 6″, but you must cut a ½″ seam allowance around the image for accurate piecing. We are working only with ½″ seam allowances in this project. Also, remember to use lightweight fusible interfacing on the wrong side of your transfer to stabilize the fabric before sewing to the heavier fabrics.

- 1 yard thin ribbon for attaching doodads

- 8 buttons, 1″ or larger

- Embellishments and/or large beads

- 2 packages of coordinating satin blanket binding

- Cotton batting: 46″ × 46″

- 1½ yards plush fleece for backing (58″–60″ wide)

Cutting

■ From each decorator print for blocks A, B, C, and D, cut 1 strip 7″ wide.

Working with 1 strip at a time, cut 4 squares 7″ × 7″ from each.

■ From each decorator print for blocks E, F, and G, cut 2 strips 7″ wide.

Working with 1 strip at a time, cut squares 7″ × 7″ from the strips. Cut 12 squares from fabric E and 8 squares each from fabrics F and G.

How-To

1. Arrange the squares and photo transfers into 7 rows of 7 blocks each (see Assembly Diagram, page 25).

2. Carefully pin and sew the blocks for each row together, *remembering your ½″ seam allowance!* Press seams *open*, not to the side.

> **tip**
>
> *I used my embellishments for the center block of the quilt. Using a ribbon or cord, I looped the metal embellishments, which are made to have a ribbon threaded through them for scrapbooking, then I slipped the ends of the ribbon between the blocks while pinning the blocks together. I made sure that the ribbon was wide enough to have its ends well secured by the stitching, and then I backstitched over the sewing to add a little more security to the stitching. Make sure the embellishments will not easily come off of the quilt!*

3. Sew the rows together, carefully pinning and matching the intersecting seams. *Remember to use a ½″ seam allowance!* Press seams *open, not to the side.* If the top needs additional pressing, use spray starch, but be careful not to spray your transfers because they may spot. Also, a pressing cloth will help to keep your synthetic fibers from scorching.

Finishing

1. Prepare the layers for quilting following the directions for Sandwiching & Basting (page 14).

2. Along each side of every seam line, stitch ¼″ from the seam. This will create a narrow plaid-type pattern and will hold down each bulky seam.

Quilt ¼″ from each seam line.

3. Stitch about ¼″ in along the outer edges of the quilt. This secures down any flimsy patch that might shift later.

4. Using your large rotary cutter and longest ruler, trim the edges even with the blocks. Working with heavy fabrics and plush backings, you should expect a little slippage here and there. I counter this by trimming my edges to the seam allowance of a corner block and use that as my guide for trimming the other 3 sides. Because the outer blocks are about 6½″ after stitching and quilting, place a ruler on the first inside seam line and cut 6½″ from that line along the edge. I may end up with a block that doesn't quite reach the edge, but it should be close enough to enclose in the binding.

5. Carefully pin the satin blanket binding to the outside edges of the quilt. Follow the directions for Binding (page 16), using a walking foot and a ½″ seam allowance instead of ¼″.

6. You will not be able to hand stitch the binding to the back of the quilt because of the fleece. Instead, pin the binding in place on the back and carefully machine sew just along the inside edge of the binding from the front, being careful to remove the pins before you sew over them. Again, a walking foot is really helpful for this step.

7. Add a label and enjoy giving comfort to someone in need!

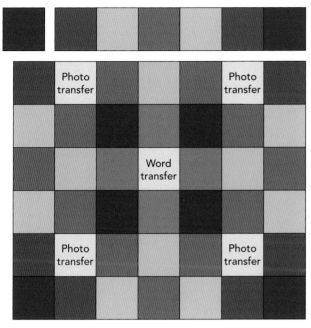

Assembly Diagram

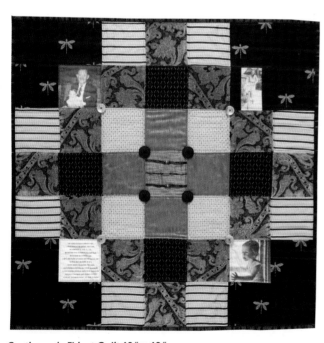

Gentleman's Fidget Quilt 42″ × 42″

I used ribbon and bead embellishments in the center block of this variation. I sewed the ends of the ribbon into the seams and then backstitched over the sewing to ensure the embellishments would not easily come off the quilt.

Chair Bound:
A Wheelchair Quilt with Footwarmer

Adult version: 36″ × 60″, Child's version: 30″ × 54″

W heelchairs present specific problems for quiltmakers. Because your recipient is sitting, a quilt designed for the chair-bound needs to be narrow enough not to catch in the chair's wheels yet long enough to cover and comfort. Using my husband as a guide, I settled on an adult-sized quilt that finishes at 36″ × 60″. It's easy enough to fold the top over onto someone's lap but still pull the quilt into a bed for warmth. The narrow size is enough to cover most people's laps and tuck under their legs to secure the edges from the chair's wheels.

My wheelchair experiences are limited to a few hospital stays and one day when I was a journalism student in college who just had to see how compliant my school was with the Americans with Disabilities Act access requirements. I spent some time rolling around campus. (Although, as the editor of the campus newspaper, I ended up spending more time assuring people that a disgruntled reader had not injured me!) As a hospital patient, my toes were always cold as I was wheeling around the hallways. So, at the bottom of this quilt, I created a foot pocket from the flannel backing fabric to keep those tootsies warm.

Like most of the other comfort projects in this book, the *Wheelchair Quilt* was designed to sew quickly and easily. It's also completely adaptable for men and women. There are so many wonderful fabrics on the market today it would be a cinch to whip up a golf quilt, sailing quilt, or car quilt for that favorite guy in your life. The same also holds true for women; there are so many beautiful fabrics to select from!

The blocks are simple and classic quilt blocks. The checkerboard rows are really just five alternating nine-patch blocks joined together, but we'll put them together in segments. The rail fence blocks are made from strips and can easily be changed or swapped out if you wish to add photos or signature blocks to the center. For the flying geese blocks, I chose paper piecing.

Many quilters are understandably intimidated by paper piecing. When I teach my students paper piecing, I tell them up front that the only way to learn the technique is to not think about why they're doing what they're doing and instead perform each step carefully from the directions. Paper piecing requires turning your thinking inside out, and that only gets in the way of making a quilt. So, don't think; just piece according to the directions. When you're done, it will all make sense, and you will have created perfect points within perfect blocks that join together perfectly! That's why it's worth learning the technique on a relatively simple block.

Finally, so many children end up in wheelchairs that I adapted for a version their size. I simply eliminated the borders from the adult-sized version, trimming 6″ off the length and width. Again, the quilt can be folded over onto someone's lap, and the extra length shouldn't get in a chair-bound child's way. But rows can also be eliminated from the quilt's construction if that's a concern.

Materials

- ⅜ yard each of 2 prints (A, B) for checkerboard rows
- ½ yard of medium print (C) for flying geese rows
- ⅝ yard of light print (D) for flying geese rows
- ¼ yard each of 2 prints (E, F) for rail fence row
- ⅞ yard of focus fabric for panel rows
- ¾ yard for border (omit for child's version)
- 2½ yards flannel for backing and footwarmer (2¼ yards for child's version)
- ⅝ yard for binding (½ yard for child's version)
- Batting: 40″ × 64″ (34″ × 58″ for child's version)
- Add-A-Quarter ruler

Cutting

- From each of fabrics A and B, cut 3 strips 2½″ wide.
- From fabric C, cut 2 strips 4½″ wide. Cut at 3½″ intervals to make 20 rectangles 4½″ × 3½″.
- From fabric D, cut 2 strips 4½″ wide. Cut at 3½″ intervals to make 20 rectangles 4½″ × 3½″. Also cut 4 strips 1½″ wide.

> **tip**
> *It's possible to use a directional print for both fabrics in the flying geese blocks, but more care will need to be given to the placement of the pieces on the pattern. Remember that the center points are positioned in opposite directions for each row. When I used the owl and feather fabrics (page 29), I double-checked before stitching each block to make sure that I had 10 geese blocks pointing to the left and 10 geese blocks pointing to the right.*

- From fabric E, cut 2 strips 2½″ wide.
- From fabric F, cut 1 strip 2½″ wide.

- From focus fabric, cut 2 rectangles 30½″ × 12½″.

- From border fabric, cut 5 strips 3½″ wide.

- From flannel, cut 1 piece 40″ × 64″ and 1 piece 40″ × 18″. (Cut 1 piece 34″ × 58″ and 1 piece 34″ × 14″ for the child's version.)

- From binding fabric, cut 6 strips 2½″ wide. (Cut 5 strips 2½″ wide for the child's version.)

How-To

Checkerboard Rows

1. Sew strips from fabrics A and B together in the following order: A-B-A. Press the seams up.

2. Sew strips from fabric A and B together in the following order: B-A-B. Press the seams down.

3. Cut the strip sets into 2½″ segments. Cut 16 A-B-A segments and 14 B-A-B segments.

4. Arrange 15 alternate segments starting and ending with A-B-A to form a row (see Assembly Diagram, page 31). Piece together, matching the intersections. Press in one direction. Repeat for the second row.

Paper-Pieced Flying Geese Rows

1. Photocopy the pattern to the right. I use standard copy paper, but if you prefer vellum or other paper designed for paper piecing, feel free to use it. Make all of your copies at the same time to avoid any distortion. You will need 20 finished geese blocks. (Print at least 22, to allow for mistakes.)

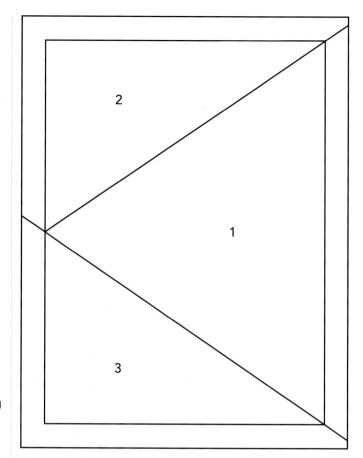

Flying geese block

2. Trim the paper pattern pieces about ⅛″ from the outside line. Do not cut right to the pattern's edge. The blocks are trimmed to size later. The pattern is divided into 3 sections. Fabric C is placed in Section 1 for the center point. Fabric D is placed in Sections 2 and 3 for the background. This is also the order in which the pieces are sewn to the pattern.

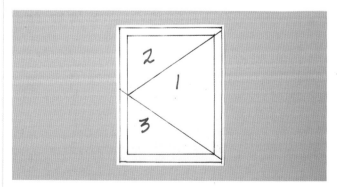

The flying geese block has three sections.

3. Cut the fabric D rectangles once diagonally to make 40 triangles. Place pairs of rectangles right sides together to cut so the triangles will be mirror images.

Cut fabric D rectangles in half diagonally.

4. With the right side of the pattern facing up, place a rectangle of fabric C on the back, right side out. From the pattern front, pin the fabric in place. Fabric C should completely cover Section 1. You can check this by holding the pattern and pinned fabric up to a light or window and making sure the fabric is centered correctly.

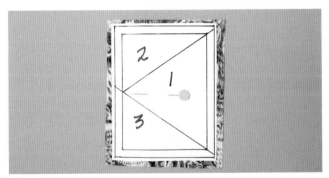

From the front, pin fabric C in place on the back.

5. Turn the pattern over so the right side of fabric C is facing up. Position the triangles from fabric D right side up in Sections 2 and 3 to check placement.

From right side, lay out fabric D triangles for placement.

6. Remove the triangle from Section 3 and set aside. Turn the Section 2 triangle so the right sides of both fabric C and the triangle are facing. Position the long edge of the triangle along the sewing line between Sections 1 and 2.

Turn triangle D right sides together to prepare for stitching.

7. Carefully move the long edge of the triangle so it's about ¼" beyond the sewing line. You can do this by turning the pattern paper-side up and watching where each corner of the triangle extends out from the edge of the paper pattern. Pin in place.

8. Shorten the sewing machine's stitch length to 1.8. The shorter stitch length will perforate the paper pattern, which makes for easier removal later. With the pattern right side up, stitch on the line between Sections 1 and 2. Start stitching at one end of the printed line and finish at the other. Don't backstitch and try not to sew off the ends of the line.

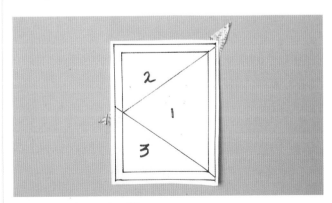

Carefully stitch on printed line.

9. Place the pattern paper-side up on the cutting mat.

10. Fold back Section 2 on the paper pattern, exposing the fabrics C and D under it.

Fold back Section 2 to expose the fabrics.

11. Position the Add-A-Quarter ruler or use your rotary ruler to measure ¼″ from the paper's folded edge and trim the fabrics. This is now your ¼″ seam allowance for this piece.

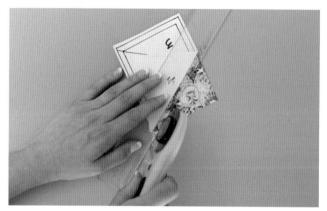

The Add-A-Quarter ruler is a wonderful tool to simplify the trimming.

12. Turn the piece fabric-side up, open the Section 2 triangle, and press with a dry iron.

Press Section 2 open.

13. Place the remaining triangle onto the pattern with right sides of fabrics together. Position the long edge of the triangle along the sewing line between Sections 1 and 3. Then, carefully move the long edge of the triangle so it's about ¼″ beyond the sewing line. Pin in place.

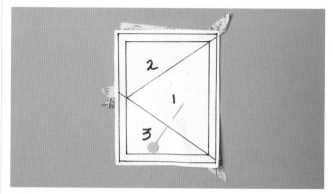

Add second triangle D to the pattern and prepare to stitch.

14. Repeat Steps 8–12. You now have a finished flying geese block. Make 20 blocks. Carefully trim the blocks to the outside line on the paper pattern using a rotary ruler and cutter.

15. Carefully remove the paper patterns from the blocks by folding the paper along the seam line and gently tearing the paper along the perforated line. Don't pull hard, or the seams could be lifted.

16. Piece together 10 blocks pointing in one direction and 10 blocks pointing in the opposite direction (see Assembly Diagram, page 31). Press the seams for each row in one direction.

17. Sew 1½″ strips to the long edges of each flying geese row. Press the seams toward the strips. Sew 1½″ strips to the ends of the rows if needed. Press toward the strips.

Rail Fence Row

1. Sew strips from fabric E and F together in the following order: E-F-E. Press the seams in one direction.

2. Cut the strip set into 6½″ sections to make 5 blocks.

3. Arrange and sew the blocks together in an alternating horizontal/vertical pattern (see Assembly Diagram, page 31). Make 1 row.

Putting It Together

1. Sew the pieced rows and the focus fabric pieces together following the Assembly Diagram. Press toward the focus fabric pieces.

2. Piece the border strips and sew to the quilt following the directions for Borders (page 14).

Finishing

1. Make a hem for the footwarmer by folding one long edge 1″ to the wrong side and pressing. Fold a second time at 1¼″ and press. Sew about 1″ from the folded edge to secure. Set aside.

2. Prepare the layers for quilting following the directions for Sandwiching & Basting (page 14). Machine quilt as desired.

3. Trim the edges of the backing and batting even with the top. Place the footwarmer on the quilt's back bottom edge, right side facing out. Trim to match the edges of the quilt and pin in place.

4. Make and attach the binding following the directions for Binding (page 16).

5. Add a label and enjoy!

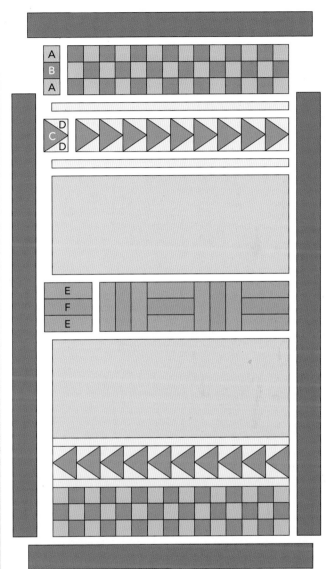

Assembly Diagram

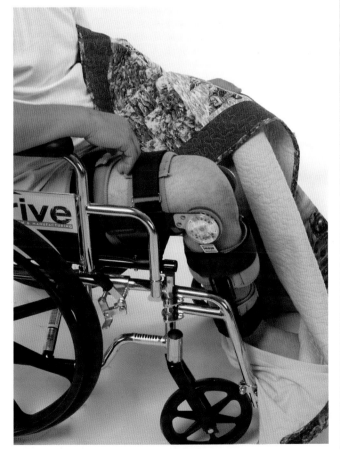

What a great place for keeping toes warm!

Vancouver Quilters Guild

Comforting the Littlest Ones:
NICU Quilts

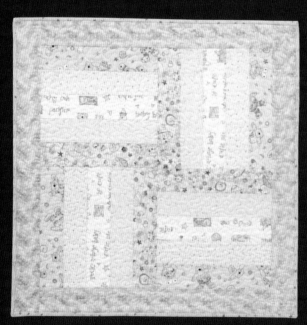

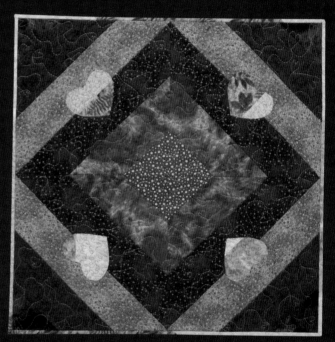

24″ squares

Making NICU (neonatal intensive care unit) quilts has become an established quilter's cause. With the recipients being our society's most innocent and vulnerable, and with the quilts' sizes being so small, it's a wonderful charity project in which individuals and groups can invest their time. You can also look beyond premature babies as recipients. These quilts make perfect gifts for young children who will latch onto these snuggly little squares of comfort. Their size makes them perfect for little fingers to drag around.

To see the infants in the NICU and the medical staff and families caring for their needs is an eye-stinging experience. Here are these tiny, fragile babies struggling to breathe and eat beyond the safety of their mother's womb, and everything in their NICU environment is dedicated to those tasks. The NICU is a quiet place. Visitors speak softly so as not to disturb the little patients. There is a constant, low hum from the machines and monitors helping the babies. Sometimes a baby will cry, and whether strong or weak, the sound is always small.

One of the things that struck me during my visits to the NICU was how it felt to stand among the isolettes containing these precious lives. Hope, fear, patience, faith, and, above all, love seemed to swirl above the babies' isolettes, blanketing them in strength and willpower. It's a place of reverence and the men and women who fight to make these young ones live, and who carry the weight of the family's prayers on their shoulders, are amazing.

Sizes for NICU quilts vary from 14″ to 36″ square or rectangular. I've settled on quilts that finish at about 24″ square. This size allows the baby to be covered but not smothered. It also allows NICU staff and parents to cover an isolette with the quilt, another factor that makes these little beauties so appreciated.

A few of the nurses I spoke with appreciate receiving pairs of matching quilts so they can cover the isolette, which protects the babies' eyes from the bright lights in the NICU, and also cover the baby. Because these are so fast to make, you can easily double up a pattern, or follow my directions below for the two quilt tops from a dozen fat quarters. For these, you'll use the leftovers from one color way for the appliqué and binding for the quilt in the other color way.

The quilt with blue circles on a green background does not have batting because the microfleece I used for the backing provides a wonderful weight for these baby quilts. The quilt with green hearts on blue background has a flannel backing, with traditional all-cotton batting between the layers. Either option works well, but each yields a different finished feel in the quilt. The microfleece backing without batting option makes the quilt very soft and huggable. The flannel/batting combination instead offers a firmer feeling quilt, one that would likely hold up better with continued washing.

In September 2000, one of my closest friends, Amy Bentley, went to her obstetrician complaining of a stomachache. Amy was 27 weeks pregnant with her only child and, thus far, had had a normal pregnancy. In less than an hour, she delivered my godson, Logan Douglas Bentley.

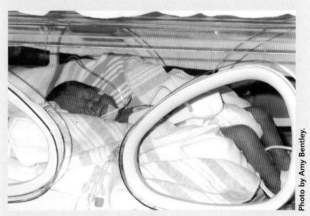
Photo by Amy Bentley.

Logan was so little in his isolette.

Born 13 weeks early, Logan was considered a "super preemie," and there was no doubt he'd spend several weeks, if not longer, in the neonatal intensive care unit. Tiny though he was (two pounds, three ounces and fourteen inches long), his medical problems were blessedly manageable in comparison to many other preemies born around the same gestation period, and he was released about seven weeks later. Today, he is a brilliant, energetic six year old with no lingering health issues beyond a mild speech delay.

Wash these quilts once they are completed. All washing should be done using a mild detergent. If you want to prewash any of the fabrics, that's fine, but know that prewashing cut strips might cause them to unravel at the edges. To offset the unraveling, use a lingerie bag to hold the fabric pieces while laundering.

Two Little Quilt Tops in About an Hour

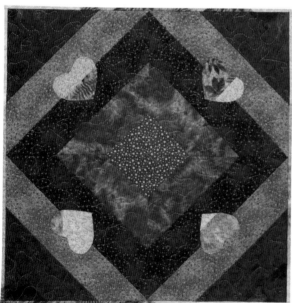

- ¼ yard lightweight fusible web

- 1 yard microfleece (or 1¾ yards flannel) for backing

- Batting: 2 pieces at 28″ × 28″ (for use with flannel backing)

Cutting

- From each of the 6 first color way fat quarters, cut 4 strips 3½″ wide. (Stack the fat quarters, trim the selvage edge, then cut strips from the trimmed edge as described on page 12.) From the leftover pieces, cut a total of 7 strips 2½″ wide for binding. Repeat for the 6 second color way fat quarters.

- From microfleece, cut 2 squares 28″ × 28″. If using flannel and batting, cut 2 squares 28″ × 28″ from each.

How-To

1. Sew 6 strips together. Repeat to make 4 strip sets.

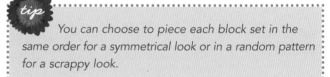

tip — *You can choose to piece each block set in the same order for a symmetrical look or in a random pattern for a scrappy look.*

2. Press the seams of 2 sets in one direction and the seams of the other 2 sets in the opposite direction.

3. Using at least a 15″ square ruler, line up the center seam of the strip set to the diagonal marking on the ruler. Then, measuring 12½″ square, cut 1 block. Keep the leftover corner pieces. Repeat with the other strip sets.

Cut blocks accurately and keep leftovers.

Materials

- 6 fat quarters of first color way for blocks, appliqué pieces, and binding

- 6 fat quarters of second color way for blocks, appliqué pieces, and binding

4. Arrange the blocks as shown in the Assembly Diagram below. Sew into 2 rows, making sure to match the opposing seams for easier piecing. Press the seams in opposite directions. Join the rows. Press the seam to one side.

5. Repeat Steps 1 through 4 for the second set of fat quarters.

6. You now have 2 quilt tops measuring about 24½˝ square. From the leftover corner pieces, cut simple shapes of your choosing from the options provided.

7. Fuse and stitch the shapes to the tops using your favorite, fast method or follow the directions for Machine Appliqué Using Fusible Adhesive (pages 13–14).

Finishing

1. Prepare the layers for quilting following the directions for Sandwiching & Basting (page 14). Quilt as desired using fun colors of thread.

2. Make and attach the binding following directions for Binding (page 16).

3. Add labels to your finished quilts and wash.

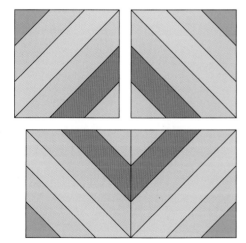

Assembly Diagram

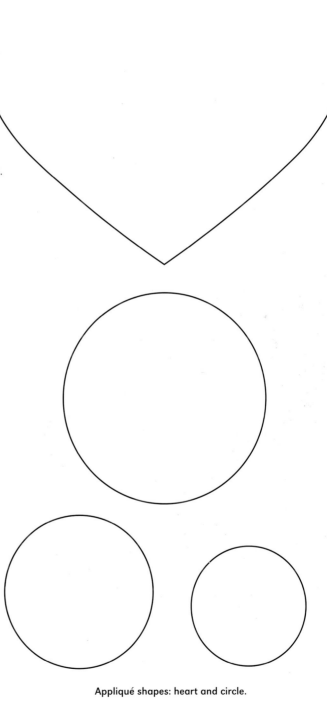

Appliqué shapes: heart and circle.

Baby Strip Quilts

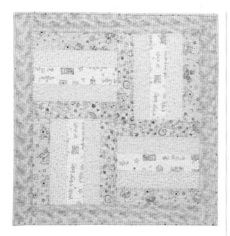

I wanted to experiment with "jelly-rolls," the bundles of 2½" strips that now are readily available in quilt shops. If precut strips aren't available, or if you want to cut strips from larger pieces of fabric, figure each ¼ yard of fabric yields at least 3 strips 2½" wide.

Materials

NOTE: *Each strip should measure at least 42" long. If it doesn't, and you simply must use the fabric, double the amount of the needed strips.*

- 5 strips 2½" × 42" (or ¼ yard each of 5 fabrics) in assorted colors for blocks
- 3 strips 2½" × 42" (or ¼ yard) of one fabric for border
- 3 strips 2½" × 42" (or ⅓ yard) of one fabric for binding
- ⅞ yard for backing
- Batting: 28" × 28"

Cutting

- From yardage, cut the number and size of strips listed under Materials.

How-To

1. Sew 5 strips together to make 1 strip set. Press the seams in one direction.

2. Trim the smallest amount possible from one end of the strip set to even up the edge. Cut 4 blocks 10½" × 10½" from the strip set.

> **tip** *If the strips are shorter than 42", you will only get 3 blocks from the strip set and will need to make an additional strip set. Sew the strips in the same order as the first strip set.*

3. Arrange the blocks in a windmill pattern as shown in the Assembly Diagram. Sew into 2 rows. Press the seams in opposite directions. Join the rows. Press.

Finishing

1. Sew the border strips to the quilt following the directions for Borders (page 14).

2. Prepare the layers for quilting following the directions for Sandwiching & Basting (page 14). Quilt as desired.

3. Make and attach the binding following the directions for Binding (page 16).

4. Add a label to your finished quilt and wash.

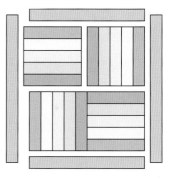

Assembly Diagram

Larger NICU Quilt Variation

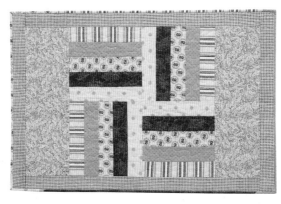

Sometimes a hospital will ask that a quilt destined for a NICU be made larger than the 24" square quilts I've offered. To make a quilt that measures 34" × 24" finished, cut 2 strips of fabric measuring 5½" × 20½" and sew to either end of the 4 joined blocks. Add 2½" borders around the entire pieced top and quilt as desired. If a hospital wants yet a larger size, adapt these instructions to their requirements. You will still have a very easy and quick quilt to make.

Cozy in Bed:
A Quilted Bed Shawl with Pockets

70" × 20"

B ed shawls are the best gifts when you're looking to make something quick and useful for another person. By changing the colors and prints of the fabrics, the *Bed Shawl* can be made for men or women, kids or adults. For the times I spent in the hospital, I was always warm enough when I was lying down in bed. But if I was wearing one of those dreaded hospital gowns, I would always chill when I sat up, either in bed or in a wheelchair. I included pockets in the *Bed Shawl* because when I was sore from surgery, the last thing I wanted to do was search for my glasses or stretch to reach my lip balm.

The featured bed shawl uses microfleece, the kind used in baby blankets, as a backing because it makes the shawl softer. With the fleece back, I used flannel as my middle layer. I have also used microsuede, which was a little more difficult to quilt, but created a soft and inviting hand when paired with a needle-punched cotton batting. Flannel is also a good choice for warmth, and regular quilter's cotton is fine, too. You want a shawl that is soft and flexible, so keep in mind how best to achieve this with whatever backing and batting you use.

The *Bed Shawl* also makes a great, fast gift project. I gave one to my beloved aunt on her 90th birthday last year. For this project, I picked shades of orange batiks because orange makes people smile and promotes healing. This *Bed Shawl* is a perfect fat quarter project!

I purchased presorted embellishment yarns that are found in the scrapbook sections of craft stores. A few different manufacturers offer these with 6 to 8 choices of fun yarns on a card. Each length needs to be about 2 yards to span the length of your shawl. Using leftover yarn from other projects is also fine. To couch the yarn, use a thread that blends with all the other colors used. This can be a fancy thread, such as rayon or metallic.

Materials

- 8 fat quarters for shawl
- 1½ yards for backing
- ⅝ yard for binding
- Batting: 74″ × 24″
- Yarns for embellishing

Cutting

- From each of the fat quarters, cut 1 each of the following sizes of strips: 4½″, 3½″, 2″, and 1½″ wide. Also, cut 2 strips 2½″ wide. (Stack the fat quarters in groups of 4, trim one long edge, then cut strips from the trimmed edge, as described on page 12.)
- From backing fabric, cut 2 pieces 24″ × the width of the fabric.
- From binding fabric, cut 6 strips 2½″ wide.

How-To

1. Set aside 2 strips 4½″ wide, to be used later for pockets.

2. Spread the strips out on the floor or a table, or hang them from a quilt rack or hanger, and randomly choose your first 2 to piece together. When choosing your strips, don't put 2 strips of the same fabric together. Vary the widths of the strips pieced next to each other.

3. Match the top edges and sew the strips together using a ¼″ seam. The bottom edges will probably not be even, but we'll trim them when we're done.

> **tip**
> If you're piecing together directional fabrics, vary the direction of the individual strips as you piece. Your bed shawl will be looked at from both angles when it's wrapped around your loved one.

4. After adding 3 or 4 strips, stop and press the seams in one direction. Liberally use your spray starch when pressing to give the strips more stability.

Stitching strips is fast and easy.

5. Continue to piece and press strips until your shawl measures about 70″ long. Press well.

6. Fold in half lengthwise, with wrong sides together. Carefully match the long edges of the strips every few inches, pinning toward the raw edges. Press in half along the length.

Match and pin long edges together.

7. Using 2 rulers if needed, measure and rotary cut 10″ away from the fold, being careful to remove pins along the way. The finished dimensions should be 20″ × 70″. Press to remove the crease at the fold.

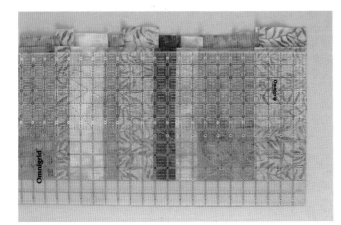

Use 2 rulers to square up shawl.

tip

If your shawl is destined for a small person or child, you can shorten the width accordingly. A child might be more comfortable with a size of 15″ × 50″. Experiment with a measuring tape and your recipient if possible.

Finishing

1. Sew the backing pieces together to form a rectangle. Trim to 24″ × 74″.

2. Prepare the layers for couching/quilting following the directions for Sandwiching & Basting (page 14).

Couching

1. Use a zigzag stitch and slightly lowered tension to start stitching over the selected yarns along the length of the shawl's top. Your needle should land on either side of the yarn as it sews its way down the length of the shawl. If the stitches are too tight, it will pull the fabric into a "channel" effect. Lower your thread's tension a little at a time to adjust for the zigzag stitching. Also, you want your zigzag to be open, not tight like a satin stitch. The point is to highlight the yarn being couched, not the stitching. Still, if you use a pretty thread, the stitching becomes its own design element. Start in the center and randomly add yarn lengths on either side of the center. Because the couching acts as the quilting to hold all the layers together, stitch strands of yarn at least every 2″.

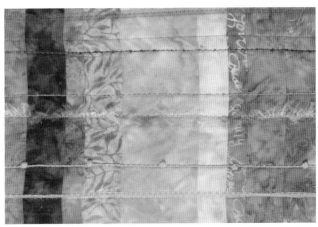

You can really have fun with the quilting on this project!

2. Make and attach the binding following the directions for Binding (page 16).

Pockets

1. Fold a 4½" strip in half crosswise, right sides together. Press and sew along the 2 long edges. Turn right side out and press.

2. Measure from the fold and cut a 7" piece to make the eyeglasses pocket. Fold under the open edge 1" for the bottom of the pocket. Center the pocket on the back of the shawl, near one end, and stitch the side and bottom edges using either invisible thread in the bobbin or a thread that will blend with the top's colors.

3. Repeat with another 4½" strip for the pocket on the other end of the shawl. Sew an additional seam down the middle of the pocket to create 2 pockets for pens or other long, thin items.

4. Create more pockets using leftover strips. Pockets could be used for small memo pads, money, tissues, lip balm, and other on-the-spot necessities when ill.

5. Add a small label to the shawl to remind the recipient of the giver.

Blue Asian Bed Shawl Variation

For the *Blue Asian Bed Shawl*, I got lazy about my couching and wanted to get the shawl done quickly. I also wanted to make the shawl look more interesting in the absence of couching. Well, sometimes my better ideas come when I'm trying to take shortcuts, and this, I think, is one of those times.

Make the pieced top of the shawl and trim it according to the preceding directions. Then carefully cut a 5½"-wide strip from both long edges. Reverse the direction of the strips and sew them to the center section of the shawl. Voilà! Here's an interesting, yet still simple, variation.

Let the Games Begin:
A Game Board Quilt

52″ × 64″

The checkers and pouch

W hat could be more fun than a quilt that you can play games with? A classic checkerboard pattern serves its intended purpose when it's centered on a lap-sized quilt and coupled with a bag of checkers. Each checkerboard square is 3″ and is quickly strip pieced. If you find your time short, the quilt can be made into a simple roll-up game board using fast2fuse and some ribbons. The directions for this variation, as well as the checkers and pouch, follow the main directions.

Materials

- ½ yard white fabric for game board
- ½ yard black fabric for game board
- ⅜ yard dark pink fabric for first border
- ⅝ yard purple fabric for second border
- 2⅜ yards flower print fabric for outer border
- 3⅓ yards for backing
- ⅝ yard for binding
- Batting: 56″ × 68″
- ⅓ yard each of light and dark prints for checkers
- ⅓ yard each of 2 prints for checker pouch
- 1 yard narrow ribbon for pouch drawstring
- ½ yard regular-weight fast2fuse interfacing for checkers

Cutting

- From both the white fabric and the black fabric, cut 4 strips 3½″ wide.
- From the pink fabric, cut 4 strips 2″ wide.
- From the purple fabric, cut 4 strips 3½″ wide.
- From the flower print fabric, cut 2 strips 10″ wide. From the length of the remaining piece, cut 2 strips 16″ × 58″.
- From the binding fabric, cut 7 strips 2½″ wide.
- From each pouch print, cut 1 circle 9″ in diameter.

How-To

1. Sew the white and black strips together, alternating the colors. Press the seams toward the black fabric.

Piece the alternating strips.

2. Cut the strip set into 8 segments 3½″ wide.

3. Arrange the segments to form a checkerboard, as shown in the Assembly Diagram. Join the segments, pressing the seams in the same direction.

Finishing

1. Sew the first, second, and outer border strips to the quilt following the directions for Borders (page 14).

2. Prepare the layers for quilting following the directions for Sandwiching & Basting (page 14). Machine quilt as desired.

3. Make and attach the binding following the directions for Binding (page 16).

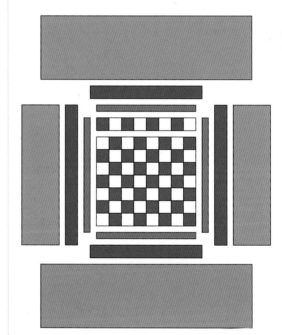

Assembly Diagram

tip

If you use a plain border fabric, the border can be turned into a friendship border where loved ones can write special messages to the recipient.

Making the Checkers

1. Fuse the light print to one side of the fast2fuse interfacing. Fuse the dark print to the other side.

2. Make a 2½˝ circle template and trace for each checker. (Note: In the game of checkers, each side has 12 checkers. I made 30 double-sided checkers to allow for losses.) Carefully cut out each checker.

Checkers are easy to make when you use a template.

Prefer Chess?

Using fast2fuse with a different fabric fused to each side, cut out these shapes in the numbers listed to create a chess game for your board.

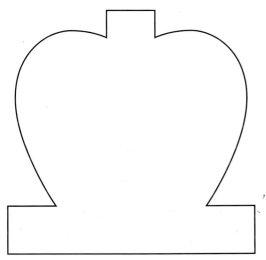

King: Make 2

Queen: Make 2

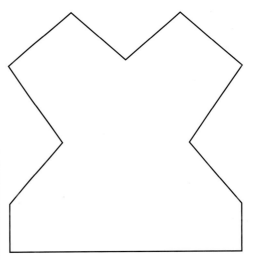

Bishop: Make 4

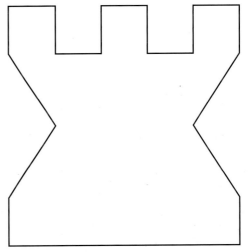

Rook: Make 4

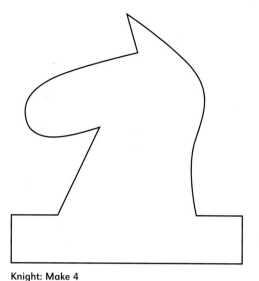

Knight: Make 4

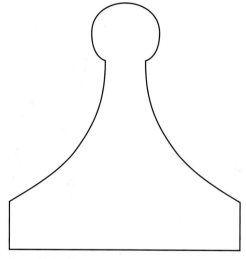

Pawn: Make 16

Making the Pouch

1. Place the 9″ print circles right sides together. Sew with a ¼″ seam allowance around the perimeter, leaving a 4″ opening.

2. Turn right side out and press. Stitch the opening closed.

3. Thread an embroidery needle with narrow ribbon and sew a running stitch about ½″ from the edge of the pouch. Tie the ribbon ends together and pull. Voilà! A bag is formed, perfect for holding the checkers or other game pieces.

tip

If you're not in a hurry, or you are concerned about unraveling, you can sew 8 small buttonholes around the edge to thread the ribbon through. Or, use 8 small grommets/eyelets along the edge and thread the ribbon through them.

Pouches are wonderful for holding all of those loose pieces.

Roll-Up Game Board

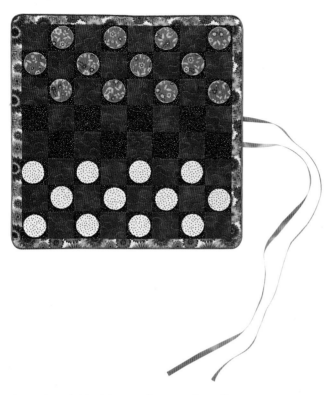

Game boards don't have to be part of a quilt.

1. Follow the directions for making the game board (page 42). Add the first border.

2. Spray baste the game board to a piece of batting 1˝ larger all around and quilt as desired.

3. Cut a ⅞-yard piece of fast2fuse to the size of the batting. Fuse a piece of coordinating fabric to the back of the fast2fuse.

4. Using your rotary ruler, mark lines every 2˝ on the wrong side of the fast2fuse and sew along each line. These lines will help the fast2fuse "roll" better.

5. Spray baste the quilted game board to the wrong side of the fast2fuse and press together well.

6. Trim the edges to the outline of the game board using a rotary ruler and rotary cutter. Then, using the cap from the can of spray baste as a template, mark and trim each corner of the game board.

7. Cut 2 pieces of ribbon 24˝ long and slip the ends between the fast2fuse and the quilted game board. Press in place.

8. Using a topstitch needle and a complementary color of rayon thread in both the top and the bobbin, carefully edgestitch around the perimeter of the game board, following the tips and techniques on page 53 for the *Walker Bag*. Be careful not to sew the ends of the ribbon together. Your board is ready to roll (sorry, again)!

Carefully edgestitch around the outside of the game board.

Roll it up when you're done!

Eye Play:
A Concentration Game Quilt

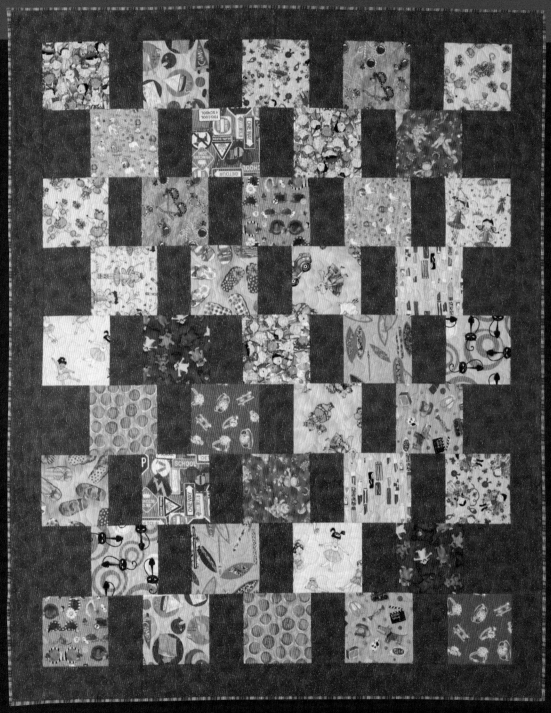

Girl's Concentration Game, 48" × 60"

I n the game of Concentration, pairs of cards are spread out and turned over, and the player has to match the pairs. This quilt, with its pairs of novelty prints, works similarly.

When my daughter was a toddler, I wanted to make her a quilt that we could use when she was sick. It had to be a quilt that would keep her occupied, one that even someone who couldn't yet read would be able to enjoy. At the time, one of my favorite catalog quilt shops was offering a packet of 6″ squares of children's novelty prints for sale. I bought two packs, separated the blue backgrounds, and created a *Concentration Game* quilt from the blocks. It has become one of our most-loved quilts, probably because I drag it to every picnic and school outing so we can sit on it, eat on it, and wrap ourselves in it, matching up the pairs of fun fabrics all the while.

This quilt quickly became a family favorite.

For this book, I made another version of my concentration quilt with the thought that a child stuck in bed would enjoy searching for the pairs of novelty fabrics included in the top. I used bunches of fat eighths found at a quilt show. Because each unfinished square of novelty print is 6½″, you only need a small amount of fabric. As there is an odd number of squares in the version, to keep it from becoming too big, I added an additional fun block of my favorite fabric. Instead, you could swap out that extra block for a dedication block where you write something for your young friend, or you could even write the rules of the concentration game on the block. It's completely up to you.

As you are selecting fabrics, try to keep the background colors in groups. In the *Girl's Concentration Game* quilt (page 46), I used only fabrics with either a pink or blue background, regardless of the print. Another option is to look for prints that have a related theme, like all bugs,

transportation, or dancers. Also, select an alternate color that serves as a neutral for all of your prints, like black or red. (If you try to match the colors in the prints, you'll go crazy!) I used a fabric that would read as a solid, one that would not compete with the mélange of novelty prints, yet that blended through color family with the novelties.

I want to thank my daughter, Samantha, for bravely letting Mommy raid her stash to acquire a couple of the novelty squares included in the quilt. I couldn't have finished this without you, Squirt!

Materials

- Fat eighth (or ¼ yard) each of 20 novelty prints

- 1¾ yards complementary colored fabric for the alternate blocks and border

- 3 yards for backing

- ⅝ yard for binding

- Batting: 52″ × 64″

Cutting

- From each novelty print, cut 2 squares 6½″ × 6½″. From one print, cut an additional square 6½″ × 6½″ for a total of 41 squares.

- From the complementary fabric, cut 4 strips 6½″ wide from selvage to selvage. Cut 3 strips at 3½″ intervals to make 32 rectangles 3½″ × 6½″. Cut 1 strip at 5″ intervals to make 8 rectangles 5″ × 6½″. Also cut 6 strips 3½″ wide for borders.

- From the binding fabric, cut 6 strips 2½″ wide

How-To

1. Arrange and sew 5 novelty squares and 4 rectangles 3½″ × 6½″ to make Row A. Press toward the rectangles. Make 5 rows.

2. Arrange and sew 4 novelty squares, 3 rectangles 3½″ × 6½″, and 2 rectangles 5″ × 6½″ to make Row B. Press toward the rectangles. Make 4 rows.

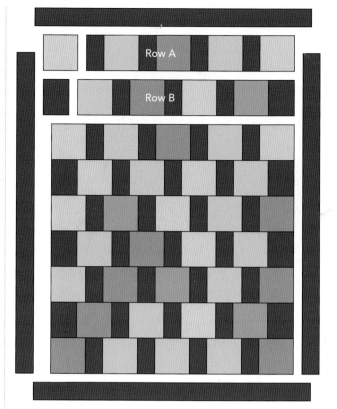

tip *I turned directional prints every which way so that the quilt could be viewed and played with from any angle.*

3. Arrange the rows as shown in the Assembly Diagram, beginning and ending with Row A.

4. Join the rows. Press the seams in alternate directions.

Finishing

1. Piece the border strips and sew them to the quilt following the directions for Borders (page 14).

2. Prepare the layers for quilting following the directions for Sandwiching & Basting (page 14). Quilt as desired.

3. Make and attach the binding following the directions for Binding (page 16).

4. Add your label and enjoy the quilt!

Assembly Diagram

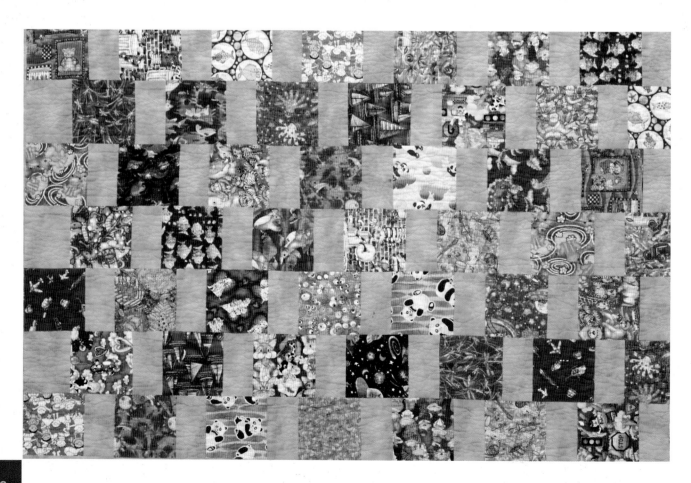

Surprise Ending:
Comfort and Fun from Two Sides

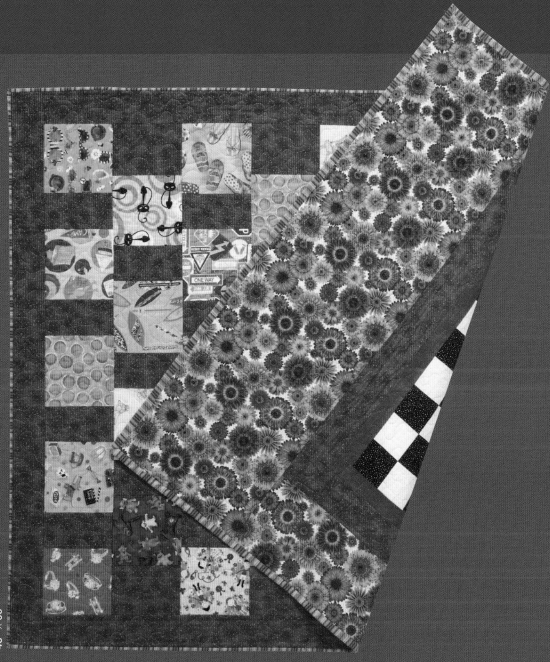

48" × 60"

kay, so I just couldn't resist a surprise ending for the *Game Board* quilt and the *Concentration Game* quilt. Besides, it saved me from having to quilt two separate quilts. If you have the time to make the two tops, creating a reversible quilt is easy. The instructions for both quilts were written with this end in mind. Your recipient will have double the fun with this gift!

Materials

- *Game Board* quilt top (pages 41–44)
- *Concentration Game* quilt top (pages 46–48)
- ½ yard for binding: Cut 6 strips 2½″ wide
- Batting: 52″ × 64″

How-To

1. Because the *Game Board* top is larger than the *Concentration Game* top, treat the *Game Board* top as the backing. Place it wrong side up and as flat as possible on your layering surface.

2. Prepare the layers for quilting following the directions for Sandwiching & Basting (page 14).

Quilting Tips for Reversible Quilts

With a quilt like this, the quilting is utilitarian and should blend into the quilt as much as possible. The best way to quilt is to use a large, random, all-over pattern like stippling. Don't try to follow the straight lines of either side of the quilt.

When choosing the thread, remember that both the bobbin and top threads will show. If your two tops have related colors, use the same thread for the bobbin and top. If you're a savvy machine quilter, using invisible thread for both the top and bobbin is another option.

The last thing to keep in mind before you begin quilting is that your machine's stitch tension needs to be accurate. Because both sides of the quilt will show, having loose stitches on one side or the other will make your efforts look sloppy and won't help the quilt's wear over time. Make a sample sandwich using the same threads, fabric, and batting, and carefully review your stitching. If the stitches look loose on either side, consult your sewing machine's guidebook and make the necessary adjustments until the stitch is right. If you just can't get the stitches to look even, your machine might need to be serviced.

Finishing

1. Carefully trim the batting and *Game Board* top to meet the edges of the *Concentration Game* top. For the straightest edge, trim using a long rotary ruler, large mat, and rotary cutter.

2. Make and attach the binding following the directions for Binding (page 16). Treat the *Concentration Game* side of the quilt as the top and the *Game Board* side as the backing.

Labeling Your Surprise Ending

Because you don't have a quilt back in a traditional sense, you can be more creative with your label. If you remember, there is an extra block in the Concentration Game quilt. You can swap out a novelty fabric for a label there. If you want to use the Game Board quilt for your label, try working the label into the border. This works especially well if you chose to use the *Game Board*'s border for signatures. Instead of making a separate label for the quilt, you can just write your label directly onto the border. That way, you don't have to worry about the label clashing with the quilt's overall design. If you do write directly onto the quilt, take the time to make your handwriting the best possible and use a wash-resistant pen such as a Pigma Micron with archival ink.

Holding On:
A Walker Bag

12" × 12"

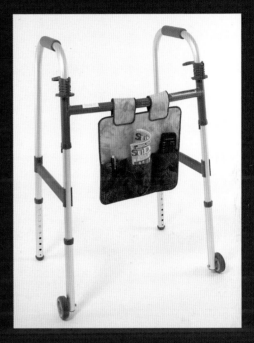

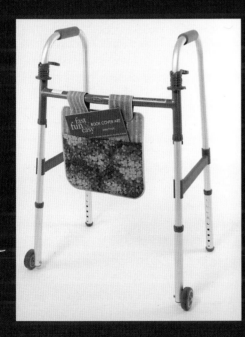

A Basket of Flowers variation

Two coordinated prints and a piece of heavyweight interfacing make up this quick and useful project. The *Walker Bag* is sized to fit most standard and specialty walkers, and the loops should fit around even the padded bars on some walkers. The finished bag can be washed, but avoid using the dryer as the heat could lift the fabric from the fusible layer.

People using walkers struggle with holding onto their personal belongings. I've watched my 90-year-old aunt wrestle with her purse or reading glasses just walking around her home. The pockets on the *Walker Bag* will hold many items, and one pocket has a pleat in it to give it more room when filled with bulkier items. Other pockets can easily be added to the original design as needed. Edgestitching, scoring, and internal facings are adapted from the techniques I developed for my *Fast, Fun & Easy Book Cover Art* projects using fast2fuse.

Materials

- ½ yard heavyweight fast2fuse (or ½ yard of non-fusible heavyweight interfacing and 1 yard lightweight fusible webbing)

- ½ yard light green for main piece and tabs

- ½ yard green print for pockets

- 1 yard lightweight fusible interfacing for pockets

- 6″ piece of hook-and-loop tape

- Appliqué pressing sheet

Cutting

- From the fast2fuse, cut 1 square 12″ × 12″ and 2 rectangles 3″ × 7½″.

- From the light green, cut 2 squares 12½″ × 12½″ and 4 rectangles 3½″ × 8″.

- From the green print, cut 2 rectangles 17″ × 13″.

- From the lightweight fusible interfacing, cut 2 rectangles 17″ × 13″.

How-To

1. Place the appliqué pressing sheet on top of your ironing board to protect the surface. Fuse a light green square to the fast2fuse square, following the manufacturer's directions. Carefully trim the fabric to the edge of the fast2fuse using scissors or a rotary cutter.

2. Fuse the other light green square to the back of the fast2fuse. Trim the fabric.

3. Repeat the same procedure to fuse the light green rectangles to the fast2fuse rectangles.

4. Fuse the lightweight interfacing to the wrong side of each pocket piece.

5. Fold each piece in half, one lengthwise and one crosswise. Press well along the fold lines to make sharp creases.

Interfacing the fabric gives the pockets stability.

6. Fold the longer pocket piece in half crosswise. Measure 1″ from the fold and pin the edges using long pins.

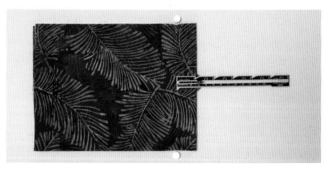

Mark with pins at 1″ along fold.

7. Open the folded piece with the pleat on top. With your fingers or a long, thin tool like a stiletto, carefully "open" the pleat evenly and press flat.

Carefully flatten the pleat with fingers. Use a long, thin tool to smooth from the inside if needed.

8. Baste across the bottom edge of the pleat. Pin the top edge to keep the pleat flat while adding the pocket to the main piece.

Sew along the bottom line of the pleat to keep it closed.

9. Center the pocket, pleat side down, on the main piece, with the folded edge 6″ from the bottom. Carefully pin in place at the corners of the pocket. Because the fast2fuse is thick, you may not be able to pin through all the layers. Just "grab" enough of the layers to keep the 2 pieces together until your basting is complete.

10. Change your needle to a fresh topstitch needle and thread the machine with rayon thread in both the top and bobbin. With the back of the main piece facing up, baste stitch about ⅛″ from the outside edge of the main piece, joining the pocket to the main piece. Your basting stitches will be covered later.

Baste pocket to fast2fuse base.

tip

You may need to adjust the tension when working with the fast2fuse. On my machine, I adjust it one step down, from 4 to 3. Before your start working on the bag, practice on a scrap of fast2fuse with fabric attached to see what tension works best. Save that scrap and write the settings your machine required to work well with the fast2fuse on the scrap.

11. Trim the excess pocket fabric to the edge of the main piece.

12. Measure 4″ from each side and mark the lines with your marking pencil. Stitch along the lines to turn the one pleated pocket into 3 smaller pockets.

13. Center the remaining pocket on the other side of the main piece, with the folded edge 8″ from the bottom. Repeat Steps 10–11 to join the pocket to the main piece.

Finishing

1. To combat the frustration of unraveling threads at corners, I round the corners using the cap from a can of spray baste or some other curved object as a template. Trace the round edge and carefully trim with scissors.

When working with fast2fuse and edgestitching, try to always round your corners.

2. Set your machine for a tight satin stitch. The stitch width should be at its widest, and the length should be at its smallest.

3. Carefully stitch around the outside edge of the main piece. To do this, your needle needs to drop off the piece on the right side of the stitch. Only the left stitch is going through the layers. The satin stitch will, in effect, bind the edges of the piece.

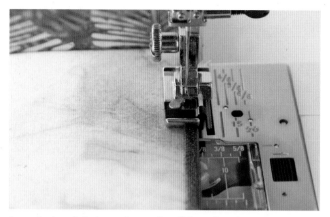

A good edgestitch drops the needle off the right side of the fast2fuse.

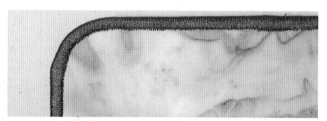

It's really just a tight zigzag stitch.

> **tip**
>
> This might take some practice to get used to, especially around the corners. Go slowly. Between the fast2fuse, 4 layers of fabric, and 4 layers of interfacing, your machine will be working hard.

4. Turn the piece over and repeat the stitching one more time. This will give your finished *Walker Bag* a professional-looking edge and will cover any mistakes made from the first pass around. If your thread gives you any trouble, change your needle.

> **tip**
>
> Many students ask if they can use their sergers for the edge finishing. A serger won't work because of the thickness of the materials it would cut through. Also, you would need to oversize the bag and then use the serger to trim the edges down, which would be unnecessarily awkward. Stick with your satin stitch. I have been able to make this work on any machine that has a zigzag stitch.

5. I "score" fast2fuse with stitching wherever I need a clean bend or crisp fold. Stitch the tabs so they will bend in the middle to hang from the walker's bar. Draw lines at the halfway point along the long edge of a tab. Then add 2 more lines, each a ¼″ from the center line. Sew on the lines. Repeat for the other tab.

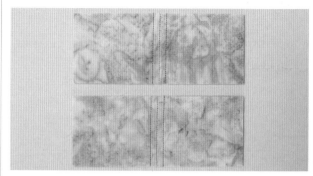

"Scoring" the fast2fuse helps it bend cleanly.

6. Using a smaller round object as a template (I use a thread spool), round the corners of both tabs, and trim.

7. Repeat the edgestitching from Steps 2–4.

8. Place the tabs 2″ from the sides and 1¼″ from the top of the main piece. Position a 2″ piece of the hook-and-loop tape on the main piece, centering it to the tab. Place the other side of the hook-and-loop tape on the tab, being careful to position it where the tab will meet the main piece to close. Repeat for the other tab.

9. Remove the tabs and sew the hook-and-loop pieces to the main piece. Sew the other side of the hook-and-loop tape to each tab.

10. Place the tabs on the main piece, joining the hook-and-loop tape together. Fold each tab over to the back to position it for sewing. Gently lift the hook-and-loop tape apart. Sew the tabs to the main piece by stitching around the inside edge of each tab.

Your *Walker Bag* is now finished!

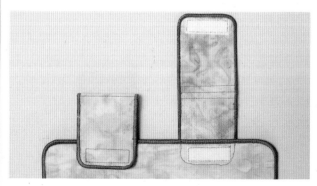

Hook-and-loop tape will keep the bag closed around the walker's bars.

Soft Touch:
A Pillowcase

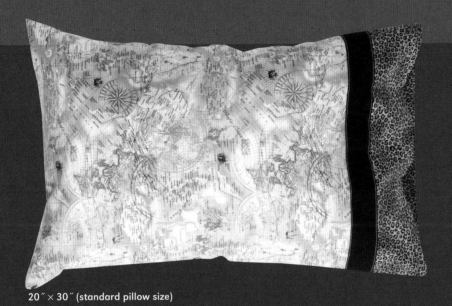

20″ × 30″ (standard pillow size)

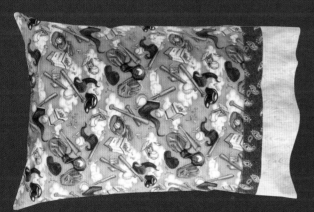

Ballgame Pillowcase

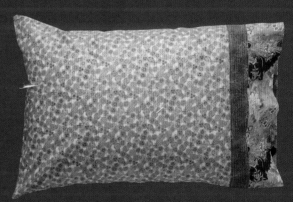

Asian Pillowcase

I don't know about you, but I always wonder about the bedding at hospitals. For that matter, I also wonder about bedding in hotels. When a loved one is in the hospital, or traveling, providing a pretty or fun pillowcase is a considerate and simple way to bring a smile to his or her face. A pillowcase is a fun and fast project that can be given alone, with a quilt, or with a stuffed animal or doll inside. You can even present your quilt inside a matching pillowcase.

Materials

- 1 yard print for pillowcase
- ⅜ yard for border
- ⅛ yard for accent border

> **tip**
> Pillowcases are especially easy projects for groups of sewers. By simply cutting your fabrics into kits ahead of time, you can assemble each pillowcase in very little time.

Cutting

- From the print fabric, cut a rectangle 41½″ × 25″. (Fold the fabric selvage to selvage and measure 20¾″ from the fold.)

- From the border fabric, cut a strip 11″ wide from selvage to selvage. Trim to 41½″ long by measuring 20¾″ from the fold.

- From the accent border fabric, cut a strip 2½″ wide from selvage to selvage. Trim to 41½″ long by measuring 20¾″ from the fold.

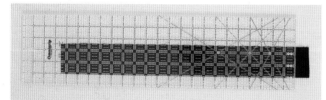

Use the length of a long rotary ruler to measure the 20¾″ length.

How-To

1. With right sides together, pin and sew the border strips together using a ¼″ seam allowance. Press toward the accent border.

2. Pin and sew the borders to the long edge of the print piece. Press toward the accent border.

> **tip**
> The technique used will "hide" the raw edges so you won't need to serge or finish the seams in another fashion.

3. Measure and fold the border at 6¾″ and press well.

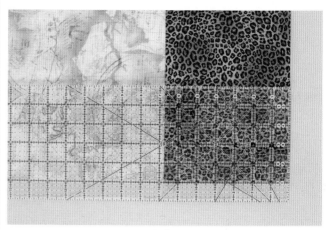

Use your rotary ruler to mark off 6¾″.

4. Open the border piece. Measure and fold the border edge at ¾″ and press well. Use a sewing gauge, found in the notions section of a fabric store, to mark the ¾″.

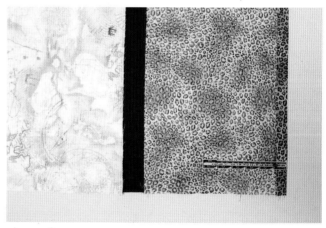

Measure ¾″ on the border edge.

5. With the wrong side of the print fabric facing up, pin the folded border in place. Then, being careful not to shift the pillowcase, turn it over and smooth the border section flat on a surface. Place several pins along the bottom edge of the accent border. Remove the pins from the wrong side.

6. Carefully topstitch along the inside of the accent border, about ⅛″ from the seam. Press well. Topstitching is a great way to highlight the lines while also stitching the border hem.

7. Carefully topstitch along the other inside edge of the accent border. You could also use a decorative stitch along this edge if desired. Press well.

Topstitch the pillowcase.

8. With *wrong* sides together, fold the pillowcase in half along the length. Pin the long and bottom edges, leaving the bordered edge open.

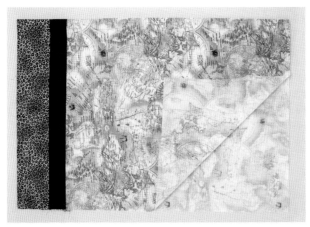

Lay your pillowcase on a flat surface to pin it correctly.

9. Stitch the edges using a ¼″ seam allowance, removing the pins as you sew.

Sew a ¼″ seam with wrong sides together.

10. Turn the pillowcase wrong side out and press the seams flat. There are some tools available to help press your unseen seams flat, but you should be able to press them well enough with your iron. Then press the pillowcase flat. Pin again along the edges already stitched.

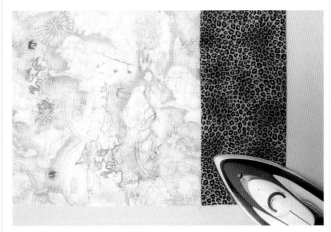

Press the seams flat.

11. Change the ¼″ presser foot to a regular foot. Stitch the edges using a ½″ seam allowance, removing the pins as you sew.

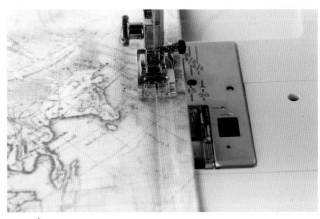

Sew a ½″ seam with right sides together.

12. Turn right side out and press one more time to finish. Your pillowcase is now ready to be put onto a standard pillow.

tip

This basic pattern lends itself well to embellishments. Just remember that the case needs to be both comfortable to rest your head on and washable. Lace and piping are wonderful insets. Sew them between the strip and border pieces.

Love Never Fades:
AN EVERLASTING BOUQUET QUILT

39" x 51"

When someone, especially a woman, is in need of a pick-me-up, flowers are a natural gift to give. When I was designing quilts for this book, I wanted to offer a fun, vibrant flower quilt that could replace the need to send flowers to someone who was sick. As a special touch, I traced my daughter's hands onto flesh-colored fabric and then used a fusible appliqué technique to adhere them to the quilt top, making it look like she was holding the flowers. You can trace your own or anyone else's hands. If the hands belong to someone dear to your recipient, how much more treasured will that quilt be?

Materials

- 6 fat quarters medium-to-dark-teal batiks for background

- 3 fat quarters bright green batiks for appliqué pieces and border

- 3 fat quarters yellow batiks for appliqué pieces and border

- 5 fat quarters total orange and red batiks for appliqué pieces and border

- 1 fat quarter flesh-colored fabric for appliqué pieces

- 1½ yards black batik for border and binding

- 1 yard lightweight fusible web

- 1¼ yards for backing

- Batting: 43″ × 55″

- Black or brown Pigma pen

- Marking pen or pencil

- *Optional: fast2cut Fussy Cutter Ruler Set: 45°-Diamond Guide (see Sources, page 78)*

- *Optional: Repositionable marking tape to mark off the 3½″ diamond on ruler*

Cutting

- From each of the teal batik fat quarters, cut 6 strips 3½″ wide. (Stack the fat quarters, trim the selvage edge, then cut the strips from the trimmed edge, as described on page 12.)

- From the black batik, cut 4 strips 3½″ wide for the inner border. Cut 5 strips 2″ wide for the outer border. Cut 5 strips 2½″ wide for the binding.

- From each of the green, yellow, orange, and red fat quarters, cut 1 strip 3½″ × 20″. From each strip, cut 5 squares 3½″ × 3½″. Set aside the remaining fabric for appliqué pieces.

How-To

1. From each stack of strips from the teal fat quarters, cut 3 diamonds at 3½″. Use the Fussy Cutter diamond guide or the 45° line on a rotary ruler. Cut at least 95 diamonds total. (Some strips may not yield 3 full diamonds. If the last diamond is minus a tip, use it for the side edge of the background, where it will be trimmed anyway!)

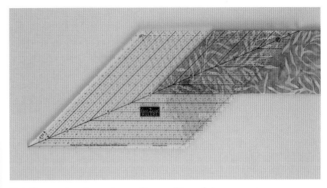

Cut diamonds using ruler or diamond template.

2. On a design board or clean surface, arrange the diamonds to form the background. The diamonds can be oriented horizontally, as in the quilt photo, or vertically, as shown in some of the following steps.

Arrange the diamonds for the background.

3. Piece the diamonds together using a ¼″ seam allowance. Match the seam lines of the diamonds, not the raw edges. Placed right sides together, the diamond tips extend beyond the diamond sides. When they are sewn and opened, the edges are straight. Press the seams in one direction.

4. Sew the diamonds together in diagonal rows, one at a time. As each row is sewn, replace it in its spot and begin the next row.

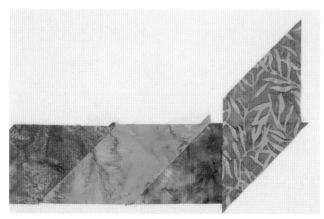

Position and sew the diamonds carefully.

5. Sew the rows together, starting from the middle and working to the outside rows. This makes it easier to handle the short rows in the corners. Make sure to match intersections carefully. This is trickier than when piecing squares with right angles, but using pins will help. Press the seams in one direction.

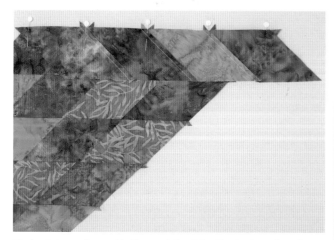

Piecing intersections with diamonds is tricky. Go slowly and use lots of pins!

6. Trim the diamond background to 24½″ × 36½″. Start with one corner and make your first cut. Line up with this edge for the other sides. It's very important to be accurate when cutting.

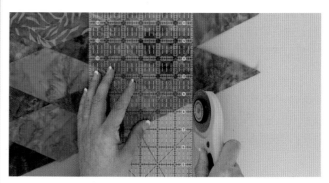

Make the first cut.

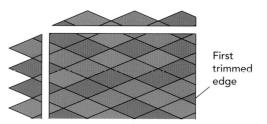

First trimmed edge

Trim the other sides.

Adding Appliqué

1. Use the technique for Machine Appliqué Using Fusible Adhesive (pages 13–14). To make the hand pattern, trace your own (with help) or anyone else's hands onto fusible web. Place the hand with spread fingers on the paper side of the web. Use a fine-line permanent marker to carefully trace from the fingers to the elbow, if possible. Roughly cut out the pieces with about a ¼″ allowance. Fuse to the wrong side of the flesh-colored fabric. Cut out the pieces on the traced lines and set aside.

2. Trace the patterns for the flowers on page 61 onto fusible web. Trace 6 of each pattern. Fuse to the wrong side of the set-aside yellow and orange batik pieces. Cut out the pieces, keeping each flower's pieces together.

A

B

C

3. Make the stems by cutting 2 strips 1½″ × 20″ from each of the set-aside green batik pieces. Press each strip in half lengthwise.

4. Using the quilt photo as a guide, position the stems, flowers, and hands onto the diamond background. The hands are "holding" the stems, so they need to be on top of the stems and flowers. The fingers are loosely intertwined on my quilt, but you can lay one hand on top of the other if you can't get them to lie flat. Remove the hand and flower pieces.

5. Place a stem on the background and pin in place at the top, middle, and bottom. Using a chalk pencil and ruler, draw a straight line along the stem's right edge for reference in case there is any shifting.

Draw a straight line where stem will lie.

6. Machine stitch ¼″ from the raw edges of the stem to about a ½″ from the bottom. Backstitch. Fold up the end of the stem.

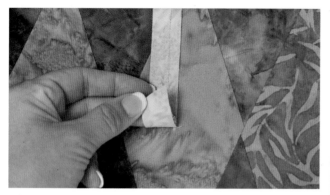

Fold up the end of the stem.

7. Press the folded edge of the stem over to cover the stitching. Press in place.

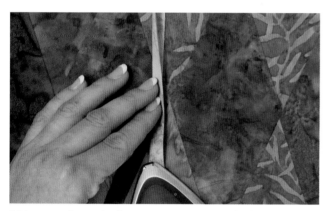

Fold stem and press in place.

8. With a decorative thread (I used light green rayon), topstitch along the folded edge to "tack" the stem in place. Sew additional lines through the stem for decoration.

Sew decorative lines through the stem.

9. Remove the paper backing from the first set of flowers. Position the pieces in order on top of the stem, covering the raw edge, and fuse in place.

Fuse the flower in place.

10. Repeat Steps 5–9 for the other stem and flower sets, one at a time.

11. Remove the paper backing from the hand pieces. Position the pieces over the stems of the flower bouquet. Make sure your placement is exactly how you want it and then fuse in place.

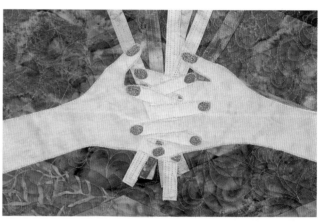

You can try to interlock the fingers for a more authentic look, but make sure the pieces lie flat before you fuse them into place.

Finishing

1. Sew the inner border strips to the quilt following the directions for Borders (page 14).

2. Arrange the green, yellow, orange, and red squares in random order for the pieced borders. Sew 2 rows of 14 squares each for the side borders. Sew 2 rows of 12 squares each for the top and bottom borders. Press the seams in one direction on all the border pieces.

3. Sew the pieced side borders to the quilt. Press to the black inner border.

4. Sew the pieced top and bottom borders to the quilt, matching the seams in the corners. Press seams to the black inner border.

5. Piece the outer border strips and sew to the quilt following the directions for Borders (page 14).

6. Prepare the layers for quilting following the directions for Sandwiching & Basting (page 14).

7. When quilting, concentrate first on the flowers and hands. I used free-motion quilting to add depth to the flowers. You don't need to be an artist to quilt decorative lines on the flowers and hands. Just have fun. For the rest of the background, I used an all-over stippling to quilt.

8. I used a Pigma pen to highlight the petals on the flowers. You can even accessorize the hands with jewelry or nail polish created from threads or fabric markers.

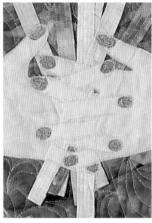

Close up of quilting on flowers and hands; the fingernails were first colored with a pink pigma pen, then freemotion stitched with pink rayon thread to fill it in. This made the nails look really pretty!

9. Make and attach the binding by following the directions for Binding (page 16).

10. Add a label and enjoy!

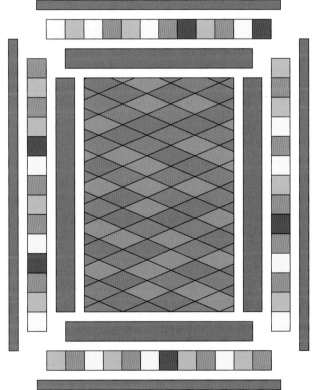

Assembly Diagram

Healing Through Words:
LABELING YOUR PROJECT

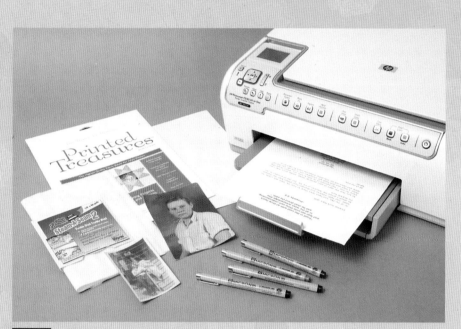

While the last step any quiltmaker should take is to label his or her efforts, a label on a quilt destined for someone ailing can have extra impact. I believe your label is the most important thing you put on your quilt.

One of the first lessons I learned as a journalist is that there is great power in words. Even the simplest words and sentences can provide great comfort over and over again for someone who is hurting. The labels you make for the back of your quilts can serve as a healing tool in its own right.

Consider, for instance, the label I wrote for my Aubrey when she was sick with cancer. I knew that the quilt I made would help to comfort her while she underwent the complicated and painful treatments used to fight her advanced cancer. I lived 300 miles away, and with a two-year-old at home, I could not be with her as much as I wanted. My prayer in making the label that went onto the back of her quilt was that when she needed it, the words I wrote for her would give her some small

measure of strength and comfort and would always let her know that she was loved.

When I made Aubrey's quilt, I was not familiar with the fabric photo transfer sheets I now liberally use. I used a plain, off-white fabric and handwrote a short letter to Aubrey on it using Pigma permanent fabric pens. I included some Bible verses to remind my young cousin that God would always be with her and that hope could be found in the most unlikely places. I also passed on some of my favorite quotes on strength and courage and my phone numbers in case she ever wanted to call me and didn't have her address book. When the quilt was finished, I slip-stitched the label to the back securely, turning the edges under to prevent fraying.

Some people recommend attaching your label before you quilt the quilt. I choose not to do this because I don't want the stitching to interfere with reading the label. If security is a concern, use fusible web, such as Steam-A-Seam 2, on the back of the label and fuse firmly to the quilt. Then, stitch around the label for added security. This is what I do with the quilts I enter in shows, and it completely bonds the label to the quilt.

Remember that labels can go on the back *or* the front of your quilt. Indeed, some of the projects in this book contain areas that lend themselves well to substituting a quilt label. The *Fidget Quilt*, for instance, can have one of its photo blocks swapped out for a label. The *Wheelchair Quilt* and the *Concentration Game* quilt can also incorporate labels on their fronts.

The only rule to follow when it comes to labels is to make sure you have one!

I have since made other quilts for people in need and whether I know the recipient or not, I always include something I hope is inspirational. When I seek comfort, I often turn to the Bible, but hope and encouragement can be found in many places, religious and secular alike. Scour quotation books and poetry for the right thing to say when you need it. Ask relatives about the recipient's reading choices and draw from there. Did you know some wonderfully wise quotes could be found in popular novels? Maybe there is a movie your recipient loves? Use a line from a much-loved movie to make them smile. The point is to know your recipient and offer words that will be understood by him or her.

tip

If you're making your quilt for a child, write your label using simple words and block letters. Many children cannot read cursive yet. Children's labels should be tailored to their ability to read and enjoy them.

*"Trust in the Lord with all thine heart,
and lean not unto thine own understanding;
in all thy ways acknowledge Him
and He shall direct thy path."*

-Proverbs 3:5

Dearest Aunt Mary Jane:

All of my life, you have been there to hold my hand and cradle my heart. Your faith, integrity and strength have always been the example by which I aimed the direction of my life. You are so precious to me, my dearest Aunt.

As you face the start of your personal battle, please know that I am there for you. I feel honored to be able to help you. Never forget that there is hope and that hope will strengthen you to prevail. You are not alone and never will be. God alone knows His plans for each of us.

All of my love,
Sarah

"No Burdens"
50" by 70"

Quilt made by:
Sarah Smith-Cooper
San Diego, California
June 2007

Given to:
Mary Jane Smith
with all my prayers for a quick and full recovery

A label can be the most important ingredient in a comfort quilt.

Hi Amber:

We know you will get better very soon. We can't wait until you're able to visit us again at the lake and we can go swimming and skip stones for miles and miles. Kevin wanted to send to you his favorite knock-knock joke. We hope you like it. Make sure you tell your mom that we are just on the other end of the telephone if you ever want to say hi! We love you, Angel Amber.

Love and giggles,
Crazy Julia, Wacky Jessica and Zany Kevin

Knock knock.
Who's there?
Boo.
Boo who?
Don't cry. It's only a joke!

A fun quilt made for Amber Allen by her cousins, Julia, Jessica and Kevin Miller (with a little help from Grandma Becky) with love and comfort.

Finished January 2006

They say laughter is the best medicine. If that's true, jokes and funny cartoons or pictures are a natural inclusion for a quilt label. Maybe you share a private joke? Triggering a personal connection through your label is a delightful way to let a person be reminded that you care.

TOP TEN THINGS YOU DON'T WANT TO HEAR IN SURGERY

1. Don't worry. I think this is sharp enough.
2. Nurse, did this patient sign the organ donation card?
3. Darn! Page 84 of the manual is missing!
4. Everybody stand back! I lost a contact lens!
5. Hand me that...uh...that uh.....thingie.
6. Better save that. We'll need it for the autopsy.
7. Accept this sacrifice, O Great Lord of Darkness.
8. Whoa, wait a minute, if this is his spleen, then what's that?
9. Ya know, there's big money in kidneys. Heck, he's got two of 'em.
10. What do you mean you want a divorce?

"The Cheer Up Quilt"
for Howard Knowles
to remind him that life is still fun...

made with love by his daughter, Penny Knowles
who learned about laughter from her beloved Daddy.
Brooklyn, N.Y.
September 2005
55" by 68"

Funny labels make people smile!

With the development of photo transfer printer fabric sheets, you can type your label into the computer, using a pretty or fun font, and simply print your note onto the fabric sheets. Before you print on the expensive fabric sheets, first print a test sheet on paper to check the ink's darkness. If it's not easy to read your label on the paper, try increasing the size of the font, changing the font, or bolding the print. Remember, the ultimate goal is to make the label as legible for your recipient as possible.

If you're giving the quilt to a child, consider incorporating pictograms. Pictograms are simple pictures used in place of words within a sentence. With the availability of clip art, it is a fun and easy label project to write out a sentence for a young one with a mix of words and pictures.

Dear Hunter:

One day, a ☺ ♟ went to ≋ where he fought a brave battle with a ⊗ ♟. Just when the ☺ ♟ thought his ⧗ was up, an angel ✈ in and rescued the ☺ ♟, bringing him to a beautiful . Sometimes we all need a helping ✋.

♥,
Mommy

A quilt made for a brave battle by Janet Wright for her son, Hunter Wright, December 2007 in Austin, Texas. We will always stand and fight together, my courageous Hunter.

Pictograms can work well for children.

You can also add photos to your label, maybe of you and the recipient or a shared location or memory you both treasure. Adding a picture might take a little more computer know-how, but there are probably friends who can help you.

Dearest Mandy,

i am always with you, especially when you think you're alone!

i love you,

Missy

An applique quilt made for a dear sister in October 2006 to let her know she is loved.
Portland, Maine

Photos can be added to any label.

Please remember to follow the manufacturer's directions on any post-printing treatment needed for your fabric sheets. It would be horrible to have your recipient wash his quilt for the first time only to have all of the ink wash off of the label. Remembering my experience when Aubrey's first quilt disappeared, you should also take a picture of both the quilt and the label for your records.

On another note about labels: I've noticed over the years that some of the recipients of my quilts, especially those mothers of children for whom I've made quilts, are borderline terrified of using a quilt because they might have to wash it. To me, there is nothing more tragic than a quilt designed to be snuggled left hanging on a wall or sitting folded neatly in a closet because the owner (or owner's mother) was afraid the quilt would be damaged.

Because of this and more practical concerns, I like to also include a second label, either attached to the quilt or in the form of a card, with wash and care instructions. All of the quilt projects in this book should withstand machine washing on a gentle cycle and air or machine drying on a delicate cycle. I would hand wash and line dry the quilts with photo transfers to preserve them as long as possible, but they should tolerate a gentle machine washing.

What Can Be Included on a Quilt Label

- Maker's name, address, and phone number
- Who the quilt was made for and why
- Name of quilt and date made
- Size and techniques used
- Personal note/letter to the recipient
- Photographs
- Jokes
- Verses and quotes
- Word games
- Poems
- Scanned cartoons
- Hand-drawn pictures
- Clip art

Vancouver
Quilters Guild

Group Effort:
MAKING COMFORT QUILTS AT LARGE

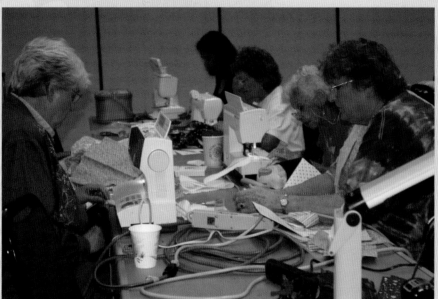

Members of the Simi Valley Quilt Guild at a September 2007 sew-in. Photo by Jake Finch.

J ust what is the best way to gather well-intentioned quilters of all skill levels to make quilts en masse? I asked the experts, those who organize quilters in groups small and large, all with the end purpose of having their quilts help others.

Local/Guild Efforts

In my home guild, the Simi Valley Quilt Guild, Nadine Coppage has led our Quilts-N-Force committee for so many years she can't remember when she started. A former guild president, Nadine leads Simi's 200 members in our annual Sew-In every March. To prepare for this event, Nadine and her team make simple kits. The kits contain the quilt pattern and instruction sheet along with all the fabric needed to make the quilt. If time allows, she might even cut the fabric as required by the pattern. While this does take considerable time, Nadine believes it allows participants to assemble more quilts.

What to Bring to a Sew-In

▨ Sewing machine in good working order

▨ Basic sewing supplies: scissors, seam rippers, extra machine needles, pins, and hand-sewing needles

▨ Neutral threads for piecing and machine quilting

▨ Rotary ruler, cutter, and mat

▨ Iron and ironing board or surface

▨ Spray baste

▨ Ott or Daylight Light

▨ Munchies to share

▨ Pajamas and slippers

(While the munchies and nighttime attire are not required to carry off a successful sew-in, it adds fun to the event and gives everyone a relaxed atmosphere in which to work.)

Divide the Labor

▨ Cutting: Someone with rotary experience

▨ Piecing: Proficient quilters with an easy working knowledge of quilt piecing (This is not the job for a beginner quilter, as working under pressure and time constraints with peers watching can cause mistakes.)

▨ Pressing

▨ Basting

▨ Quilting: Someone with machine experience

▨ Binding

▨ Labels: Consider printing ready-made labels with the guild's information, including an address (you may actually hear from your anonymous recipient) and care instructions, as many people are afraid to use your loving efforts for fear they will ruin them in the wash.

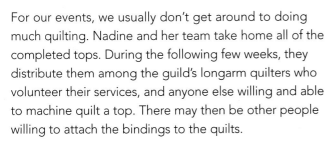

For our events, we usually don't get around to doing much quilting. Nadine and her team take home all of the completed tops. During the following few weeks, they distribute them among the guild's longarm quilters who volunteer their services, and anyone else willing and able to machine quilt a top. There may then be other people willing to attach the bindings to the quilts.

Even though Nadine isn't looking to make quilts from start to finish during a Sew-In, she will often bring quilt tops that have been donated during the year and will designate members as that night's quilters. So, she's not just concentrating on the new stuff; she's clearing out all of her existing charity inventory, which can be extensive at times with many of our members solely devoting their quilting efforts to comfort quilts. She also will distribute kits to members a month or two before the event. She encourages those quilters to return the tops at the Sew-In to allow another member to quilt it.

On a good night, the guild can count about 40 quilts made or at least significantly completed. Usually, our quilts are given to organizations within our local area of Ventura County, California. But we've been known to ship quilts out to mass relief efforts, such as the 2005 Hurricane Katrina victims. Some of the local organizations receiving our quilts include police and fire departments (with an emphasis on children's quilts), emergency rooms, women's shelters, the Alzheimer's Association, neonatal intensive care units, military families, special organizations working with sick children such as Paul Newman's Hole in the Wall Gang camps, the Ronald McDonald House, Project Linus, and cancer wards. Also, many of our members regularly make quilts to be auctioned at large events to raise money for local schools and charities. Each year, the Simi Valley Quilt Guild donates about 100 quilts made by our guild's members.

After years of working through the kinks of groups making quilts to give away, Nadine has some tips to share.

About the Process

- **Use the best possible quilting fabric.** Just because a quilt is being given to a stranger doesn't mean the end product should be of any less quality. Most of the fabrics used by Quilts-N-Force are donated; too many times, members seem to be purging their stash of the oldest and most offensive contents, which have included polyester, cotton blends, and other unusable offerings.

- **Make the quilt pattern as simple as possible.** The level of expertise among quilters can vary greatly, and everyone should be able to participate in a charity event.

- **Use good-quality batting.** Long ago, our guild used dense polyester batting in the charity quilts. Regardless of how well the tops were pieced, the quilts just didn't look as good. Now Nadine buys huge rolls of Warm & Natural using discount coupons from large fabric retailers. One bolt of Warm & Natural can be used in about 40 quilts.

- **Appreciate everyone's willingness to help and find them a task.** Anyone participating in a charity effort should be respected for donating time and effort. Every person wanting to help should be able to participate. More experienced quilters could buddy up with newer quilters. Fix mistakes discreetly so as not to hurt feelings. We are all just trying to help others, and fellowship becomes the wonderful by-product of our work.

Larger Efforts

There are basically two ways in which quilts are used for charity efforts. The first is when a quilt is made and given to a recipient or organization. In this case, the quilt is the form of charity.

The second is when quilts are made—usually from a challenge or with prescribed guidelines of theme, size, or materials—for display. These quilts are shown, sold, or auctioned (sometimes all three), and the money is then donated to an organization or group needing help.

I'm going to touch on both of these efforts and hope that I provide a starting point for anyone wanting to help others at this level. To gather the information provided, I went directly to quilters who have headed these efforts. There is a lot of work involved in setting up a large-scale effort, but it can be a rewarding undertaking. Don't be discouraged.

Quilts Made for Others and Gathered Nationally

Making quilts for national charities is not too different from a guild sew-in night. All of the tips offered above apply here as well.

There are many, many groups out there making quilts for soldiers and their families, sick children, the homeless, elderly people, victims of natural disasters, women's shelters, kid's camps, hospitals, rest homes, babies . . . the list goes on and on. A simple Internet search will offer hundreds of groups whose sole purpose is to make quilts for those in need. Almost every group I've seen, from The Home of the Brave Project (providing quilts for fallen soldier's families) to the well-established Project Linus (quilts for sick children), streamlines its efforts into quilts going to a specific recipient. With that starting point in mind, the quilt's requirements can be channeled into a simple set of guidelines that almost any quilter or sewer should be able to follow.

For instance, if you are making quilts for children, you need them to be sized for children—smaller than an adult's quilt but larger than a baby's quilt. At the Association of Hole in the Wall Camps, a group of eleven camps throughout the world catering to seriously ill children and founded by the actor Paul Newman, quilts are made for the twin-mattress-sized bunks that the kids sleep in while at camp. The camps also ask for pillowcases for the bunks. These are quilts destined for children, and the brighter, more fun fabrics work wonders to cheer a tired body.

In another example, the Home of the Brave creator, Don Beld, decided to make quilts based on one of seven surviving quilts from the Civil War era that were used to cover injured soldiers. The colors are red, white, blue, and tan in muted tones, reflecting the time period from which they came. The original quilt effort in the Civil War was coordinated by the U.S. Sanitary Commission, a fore-runner of the American Red Cross. The 48″ × 84″ quilts were used as soldier's bedrolls and on cots in military hospitals. Often, soldiers were buried in the quilts, as there was a shortage of coffins during the war. Modeled after their historical forebears, today's Home of the Brave quilts are given to the families of soldiers who have died in Operation Enduring Freedom and Operation Iraqi Freedom.

Considerations When Undertaking a Large-Scale Effort to Make Charity Quilts

- Is the need strong?

- Is the quilt simple to make?

- How will I connect with people willing to help? (See "Getting the Word Out" on page 73.)

- Do I have volunteers to help?

- Do I have storage room for the quilts until they are distributed?

- Do I need to work with the post office on delivery details when receiving quilts or materials at home?

- Do I have storage room for raw materials if I'm supplying them to others?

- What kind of records do I need to keep for a charity effort? Consult an attorney and an accountant, at the least. If you're a guild member, you might be able to tap into some pro bono advice through your guild or a regional guild organization in your area.

- Do I need to form a charity organization for tax purposes? If so, how do I go about it?

- Do I need special insurance?

- How will I handle any monetary donations that may come in?

- How will I decide on the quilts' distribution? (Easy to answer if they're all going to the same place, such as a hospital or police department.)

- For how long should this effort be in effect? In the case of soldiers' quilts, you're probably looking at the duration of the armed conflict, if that's your target recipient. If you're talking about a women's shelter, the need will continue as long as the shelter is operating.

- How much time do I have to give to this effort? All of the organizers I spoke with were amazed at how much time it took to head a charity effort. Don't be discouraged, but do be realistic. You may decide you need lots of help from the start.

- How much money can I give to the project? From phone calls to websites and postage, there will be costs involved. You need to be able to support your project until it can support itself.

- Are their sponsors or grants available to help with the costs and/or labor?

- Am I organized?

- Does my recipient group even want quilts?

- Do I know anyone who has undertaken a similar cause from whom I can draw on her experiences?

- Is photography needed to show the quilts on a website or for print brochures? If so, do I have the skills or know someone who does?

- Is my family supportive? This might be the most important question. If you're launching into a project that eats up lots of your time, your family has to be on board with it or there will be problems.

I haven't covered everything, but this list will give you a good starting point to evaluate what you can handle and where your idea can go.

Don said that when he started the Home of the Brave project, his goal was simply to make a dozen quilts to be given to the families of the fallen soldiers from his area in Southern California. He garnered lots of support from his guild and others who heard about the project. Three years later, he has a slew of area coordinators who track down the families and coordinate the sewing efforts of others. Don said that from the start he knew he didn't want his project to become a non-profit group. Instead, he wanted to keep the administration end of the project as simple as possible so as not to take anything away from the quilter who devoted his or her time to making the quilt. He opted to absorb what costs there were for shipping, materials, and so on, at the cost of several thousand dollars from his pocket.

Still, when asked if he would do this again, 2,500 quilts later, he is emphatic in his answer. "We constantly get emails and thank you letters or we talk to the families in person, and their appreciation and gratitude are all the reward that any of us need. They're an amazing bunch of people."

Money-Raising Quilts

As of late 2007, there were several major fundraising efforts underway where quilts were being made and sold to benefit Alzheimer's disease research, cancer research, and other serious diseases. Looking at two examples of these fundraisers can offer some great lessons in creativity and carrying out a mission.

Ami Simms, art quilter extraordinaire and the daughter of an Alzheimer's patient, started her effort, The Alzheimer's Art Quilt Initiative, to raise money for research. On her website, *www.amisimms.com*, she says that she started the initiative in answer to her mother's Alzheimer's she explained, "I think it is possible to make a difference, one quilt at a time."

The initiative has two parts. The first is a three-year traveling art quilt exhibit called "Forgetting Piece by Piece," which includes 52 art quilts made by some of the quilt industry's leading names, who donated their efforts to help Ami's. The exhibit goes to shows, galleries, and any other event possible and draws attention to the pain

of Alzheimer's disease through the art quilt medium. Besides seeing the quilts, viewers can also opt to buy a book and/or CD of the exhibit. All of the profit from the sales is donated to Alzheimer's research.

The second part of Ami's effort is called "Priority: Alzheimer's Quilts." These are quilts made no larger than 9" × 12" so that they fit into the U.S. Post Office's priority mailer shipping box. In the effort's first 21 months, 880 quilts have been auctioned on Ami's website, raising tens of thousands of dollars for Alzheimer's research.

"This disease touches everybody," Ami says. "If you know somebody with it, you know how devastating it is. For the Priority quilts, it's such a small time investment. It's turned into a way to cope with the sadness and do something positive that's doable."

Altogether, Ami's work—and that of the hundreds of quilters wanting to help—has raised almost $100,000. Her goal is to raise $500,000 by 2009.

"This sucks every ounce of energy out of me," Ami says. "I have never worked so hard in my life. I do nothing but this all day long. I'm working 40 hours a week on this. But it's a good thing. And it's the best work I've ever done."

Both of Ami's fundraisers are completely Internet driven. All contact is made over the Net, and information about the projects is easily accessed from her website.

When Virginia Spiegel decided to help her sister's Relay for Life team in Forest Lake, Minnesota, in its fundraising efforts on behalf of the American Cancer Society, she made seven fiber-art postcards. Her goal was to sell at least three and donate $90 to the ACS.

Two and a half years later, Virginia has raised an astounding $130,000 for the ACS.

A full-time mixed-media artist, Virginia decided on 4" × 6" fiber-art postcards. They are small, easy to make, and can be created from any type of fiber—cottons, velvets, synthetics—and can be embellished or not.

Virginia is involved in several online art quilt groups. When her art quilt friends heard about what she was doing, they began sending her postcards to sell. Her biggest pushes came first from an article about her efforts and a reader challenge in *Quilting Arts Magazine* that brought in scores of postcards from quilt artists around the world, which raised $10,000.

Then, Karey Bresenhan, the founder of the International Quilt Festival—and a breast cancer survivor herself—invited Virginia to display and sell the postcards at the 2005 festival. This four-day event raised another $20,000.

"The postcard project wouldn't have raised half or even a quarter of the money without Karey's involvement. She was really our fairy godmother. She just made it happen," Virginia says.

The experience taught Virginia many things, and she shares some advice with anyone considering a large-scale endeavor. "I would say there are two things to know. One, it has to be a labor of love because otherwise you'd be crazy to start it. And two, it does cost money. I decided it would be my donation. I paid to go to all of the conferences."

Getting the Word Out

For any charity effort that will stretch beyond the boundaries of your immediate clutch of quilters, the only way to garner support is to be able to tell people about what you are doing, why, and what you need.

Luckily, we live in an age of easily accessible information and rising quilting popularity. Between the too-many-to-count quilt magazines, other publications, and the Internet, there are many avenues to getting your needs out to the quilting world.

Somewhere along the line, written materials about what you're doing should be developed. If you're looking to approach a publication, such as local newspapers or national quilt magazines, a press release is a must. In a nutshell, and you can access more detailed information online or in public relations/marketing reference books, a press release includes the following:

- Name of group or person to contact, with at least two phone numbers

- What the project is

- Who it benefits

- Where it happens

- Why it was undertaken

- When it was started and how it's doing today (The most current happening is what's called a "news

peg." All publications look for the most current information to highlight, so if you've hit a milestone, it would be cause to send out the word.)

- Who you or your group are

- Some background on the effort so far: money raised, quilts donated, and so on

- Contacts for project benefactors, if there are any easily found (For instance, if you've given quilts to a police department, who can be contacted there about the quilts?)

If you're working directly with a specific charity or group, they might have someone on staff who can write or help with the press release. If they don't, have someone you trust read it over for mistakes. You should always have several copies available, should someone from the media contact you unexpectedly.

Another word about working with the media: Know who you're sending your information to and don't be shy about making follow-up phone calls. As a newspaper journalist, I, too often, have seen press releases land on the wrong desk or get sent to the garbage by accident. Make a phone call to the publication first, even if it's a big national magazine, and ask which editor should receive your notice. Then send it there, by mail, fax, or email (they will usually tell you how). Finally, make sure to call a few days later. The phone call will trigger greater interest on the editor's part and will help personalize your cause. The editors' job is to handle information. They want to know what you're doing, even if they choose not to publish something on the effort.

Besides a press release, photos of the project's results (quilts, postcards, or other items) should be in your arsenal of information. Also, a brochure or flier about your project is helpful when someone other than a member of the media wants to know what you're doing. If you're strictly working through a website, all of these items can be translated into web pages that anyone can access by going to your site. The information is the same, regardless of whether it's printed and handed out or searched for on the Internet.

Here is a list of free places to get your word out to and get help from:

- Scout troops (Community service projects are always being sought, and your quilt might just be the thing for a group of dedicated kids to tackle.)

- Senior centers

- Teen centers

- Service organizations like Rotary International (These groups are always looking for ways to help other groups carry out their charity efforts. You could partner with them for a community event or fundraiser that benefits both groups. You could also adapt a trunk show for their meetings.)

- Schools for all ages

- Places of employment (Gather a lunchtime group of co-workers to help make quilts.)

- Newsletters

- Community bulletin boards at coffee shops, libraries, civic centers, and other places

- Articles in local newspapers and magazines

- Articles in national newspapers and magazines

- Guilds, guilds, guilds (Think of doing a trunk show with some of your samples and offer to speak for free to a guild before a main program. Make sure you have plenty of publicity materials on hand for anyone interested in helping.)

- Quilt shows

- Volunteer listings in area publications

- Websites, chat rooms, and blogs belonging to others (Ask if they would put a link from their site to yours for the effort.)

- If you're looking to communicate through a website, make sure you know how to develop one or can tap into someone else's experience. Look at similar websites devoted to charity quilt efforts and make a list of what you like and what doesn't work. Then use that research to develop your own site. I admit I know very little about creating websites, but I know when I go to a site that's well-designed, has all of the information I need to find on it, and allows further contact with the group I'm reading about, I'm a happier volunteer. There are tons of books on the market about making websites, and many web companies offer painless programs to develop your own site.

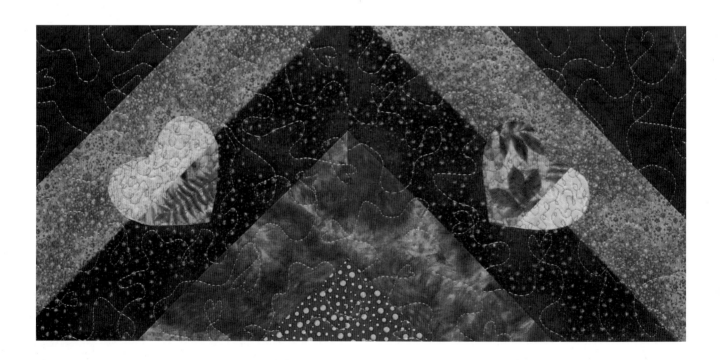

Who Needs the Help?

T he following list is merely the tip of the iceberg of organizations and individuals making quilts to benefit others.

About: Quilting

quilting.about.com

About: Quilting is an online forum for quilters that is run by author Janet Wickell. Janet hosted a sew-in event at Quilt Fest in 2007, where members from the forum met to make quilts. Efforts coordinated online between members to make charity quilts have also met with success. To access several opportunities to meet with other quilters online and help in a charity quilt effort, go to the Our Community page and scroll down to Community Projects & Quilting for a Cause.

Alzheimer's Art Quilt Initiative

www.amisimms.com

Ami's project includes "Priority: Alzheimer's Quilts"— small art quilts, no more than 9″ × 12″ that are donated to Ami, who then auctions the quilts over her website each month. All profits earned from the sales of the Priority quilts is given to Alzheimer's research.

Habitat for Humanity International

121 Habitat Street

Americus, GA 31709-3498

(229) 924-6935, ext. 2551 or 2552

publicinfo@habitat.org

www.habitat.org

Since 1976, Habitat for Humanity has built more than 225,000 homes throughout the world, providing housing for more than one million people. While the organization does not directly solicit quilts for their homes, I know that in my county, several guilds have committed to providing quilts for each bed in every new Habitat home built.

Hole in the Wall Camps

265 Church Street—Suite 503

New Haven, CT 06510

(203) 562-1203

www.holeinthewallcamps.org

The administrative organization heading 11 camps serving severely ill children, Hole in the Wall Camps was founded in 1988 by actor Paul Newman. The camps, which are located throughout the United States and over-seas, always need quilts and pillowcases for the campers' bunks. The main website provides links to each camp, which in turn has wish lists for the camps' needs.

Home of the Brave Quilts

www.homeofthebravequilts.com

quiltnweave@homeofthebravequilts.com

marianmabel2007@yahoo.com

http://groups.yahoo.com/group/Operationsupport/

Don Beld, founder of the Home of the Brave Quilts project, was not directly involved with the formation of this website. However, he does consider it the primary website for the project. Home of the Brave Quilts provides a quilt to every family who has lost a U.S. service man or woman in Operation Enduring Freedom or Operation Iraqi Freedom. After three years, about 2,500 quilts have been given away across the nation.

Marine Comfort Quilts

www.marinecomfortquilts.us

Founded by two Marine moms, Marine Comfort Quilts was initially focused on making and giving quilts to the primary next of kin who lost a Marine in the Iraq War and related Middle East operations. Recently the group expanded its purview to include fallen soldiers from any U.S. military branch. Quilts are made from 30 squares of fabric, 28 of which have handwritten messages of comfort and gratitude for the families receiving them. Donations of fabric, finished quilts, and money for shipping expenses are welcomed. So far, more than 3,000 quilts have been made or are being made for the families of fallen soldiers.

The AIDS Memorial Quilt—The NAMES Project Foundation

637 Hoke Street NW

Atlanta, GA 30318-4315

(404) 688-5500

info@aidsquilt.org

www.aidsquilt.org

Since 1987, the AIDS Memorial Quilt project has gathered panels to remember those who have died from AIDS-related complications. This ongoing project still accepts memorial panels. The finished panels must measure 36″ by 72″. Detailed information is included on the website on how to make the panels. More than 40,000 panels have been made for the quilt, which is displayed at the NAMES Project Foundation headquarters in Atlanta, Georgia.

Operation Kid Comfort

ASYMCA of Fort Bragg/Pope AFB

208 Thorncliff Drive

Fayetteville, NC 28303

(910) 436-0500

operationkidcomfort@gmail.com

operationkidcomfort.blogspot.com

Since February 2003, when a grandmother decided to make a quilt to console her grandson while his military father was deployed overseas, Operation Kid Comfort has provided personalized quilts for children whose parents are serving overseas in the U.S. military. These quilts include photo transfers of the child's parent.

Prayers and Squares International

3755 Avocado Boulevard #248

La Mesa, CA 91941

www.prayerquilt.org

Started in Southern California in 1992, Prayers and Squares makes tied quilts for anyone in need. As the tie is made in the quilt, a prayer is said for that tie. Currently, there are 687 chapters located in the United States, Canada, and internationally.

Project Linus National Headquarters

P.O. Box 5621

Bloomington, IL 61702-5621

(309) 664-7814

www.projectlinus.org

Since 1995, more than 2.2 million blankets and quilts have been donated to children who are ill or severely traumatized. There are 406 chapters covering every state in the United States.

Quilts for Comfort

Edna Kotrola

P.O. Box 592

Delaware City, DE 19706

(302) 834-1227

www.quiltsforcomfort.com

Based on the East Coast, Quilts for Comfort started in 1999 as a local effort to make quilts for elderly persons and ill children. Edna hosts regular quilt bees where anyone interested in helping to make these charity quilts can lend a hand. To date, more than 250 bees have been held to make more than 5,000 quilts.

Quilts for Kids

11 Effingham Road

Yardley, PA 19067

(215) 295-5484

www.quiltsforkids.org

Quilts for Kids' mission is to take in unwanted, outdated fabric from fabric manufacturers and designers that would otherwise be thrown away and turn the fabric into quilts for children suffering from severe illnesses or trauma. During its first five years, from 2000 to 2005, founder Linda Ayre estimates more than one million pounds of fabric saved from landfills and more than 40,000 quilts were made and given to children with AIDS, cancer, and other life-threatening illnesses, as well as those children who have been abused and neglected. There are currently about 50 chapters covering 29 states and the Bahamas, as well as a cyber chapter that operates on the Internet.

Quilt Pink

www.quiltpink.com

Created by American Patchwork & Quilting magazine, Quilt Pink is an annual effort to create quilts to be auctioned for the benefit of breast cancer research. Quilts shops across the country are recruited to host Quilt Pink events, where quilts are made and given to Quilt Pink. Those quilts are then auctioned on eBay. The 2006 Quilt Pink campaign resulted in more than 4,000 quilts being made. Quilt Pink's website offers a kit for hosting a Quilt Pink event at local shops.

Besides these national efforts, you can find many established opportunities in your own community for helping people through the gift of quilts. Local guilds are the best place to start, as many of them already have philanthropic programs in place. Area hospitals and rest homes are always willing to take in quilts for the people they serve.

Here is a potential list of recipients for any quilts you might make:

- Veteran's homes
- Hospitals
- Long-term care facilities
- Hospice groups
- Visiting nurses
- Women's shelters
- Homeless shelters
- Police departments
- Fire departments
- Rehabilitation homes
- Foster care agencies
- Food banks
- Churches and temples
- Scout troops (who then send the quilts on to others in need)

The materials used in this book were all easily located at area quilt, scrapbook, and craft stores, including online sources. Companies can also be contacted directly for orders or retail referrals.

Aurifil Threads

500 North Michigan Avenue— Suite 300

Chicago, IL 60611

www.aurifilusa.com

Adobe Elements

www.adobe.com

C&T Publishing

Makers of *fast2fuse Double-Sided Stiff Interfacing* and the *fast2cut Fussy Cutter Ruler Set: 45°-Diamond Guide*

P.O. Box 1456

Lafayette, CA 94549

(800) 284-1114

www.ctpub.com

CM Designs

Makers of **Add-A-Quarter** rulers

7968 Kelty Trail

Franktown, CO 80116

(303) 841-5920

www.addaquarter.com

J.T. Trading Company

Makers of **505 Spray and Fix** (spray baste)

458 Danbury Road

Unit A18

New Milford, CT 06776

(800) 350-5565

www.sprayandfix.com

Janome

Makers of the wonderful sewing machines that I use every day

(800) 631-0183

www.janome.com

Milliken

*Makers of **Printed Treasures** photo sheets*

(866) 787-8458

www.printedtreasures.com

Robison-Anton Textile Company

Threads for machine embroidery and quilting

P.O. Box 507

Mt. Holly, NC 28120

(800) 847-3235

www.robison-anton.com

Schmetz

This site has a cross reference for what needles work with what threads and fabrics.

www.schmetz.com

Superior Threads

*Makers of **Libby Lehman's The Bottom Line** thread. This website has an excellent reference for thread types and needles.*

87 East 2580 South

St. George, UT 84790

(800) 499-1777

www.superiorthreads.com

Timtex

Timber Lane Press

(800) 752-3353 (wholesale only)

qltblox@earthlink.net

The Warm Company

*Makers of **Steam-A-Seam 2** and **Warm & Natural Batting***

(800) 234-WARM

www.warmcompany.com

For a list of other fine books from C&T Publishing, ask for a free catalog.

C&T Publishing, Inc.

P.O. Box 1456

Lafayette, CA 94549

(800) 284-1114

ctinfo@ctpub.com

www.ctpub.com

C&T Media Services

C&T Publishing's professional photography services are now available to the public. Visit us at www.ctmediaservices.com.

For quilting supplies:

Cotton Patch

1025 Brown Avenue

Lafayette, CA 94549

(800) 835-4418

CottonPa@aol.com

www.quiltusa.com

Note: Fabrics used in the quilts shown may not be currently available as fabric manufacturers keep most fabrics in print for only a short time.

Jake has ridden the brilliant roller coaster of quilting for almost 20 years. Drawn first to the colors and feel of the fabric, she relishes each new learned skill that helps to make her quilts better. As a writer, photographer, and quilt teacher and designer, Jake has been blessed to earn a living doing what she is most obsessed with—quilting. She often wonders if she'll tire of the fabric creations, but concludes that if it hasn't happened yet, it isn't likely to in the future. This is good because there's always more fabric to buy!

Feeling like she is often on a mission to convert the masses to quilting, Jake is available for teaching and guild lectures. Her style is fun, casual, and nurturing. Allowing students to enjoy the process of creating something beautiful is more important than the finished result. Skills can be learned. Passion can only be felt.

A native New Yorker who has also lived in Alaska, Jake now lives in Simi Valley, California, with her husband, Stephen; their delightful daughter, Samantha; and their assorted cats. She can be contacted through her website, *www.jakefinchdesigns.com*.

Great Titles
from

C&T PUBLISHING

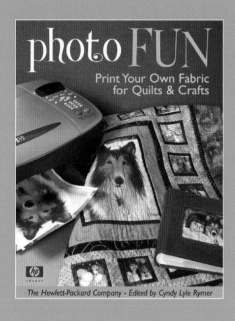
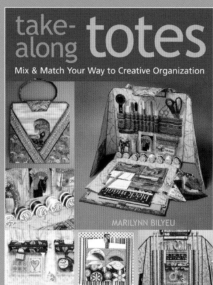
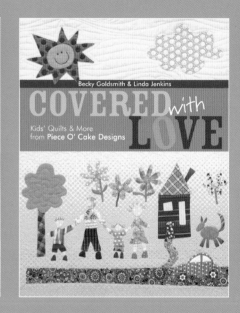

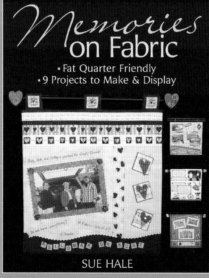
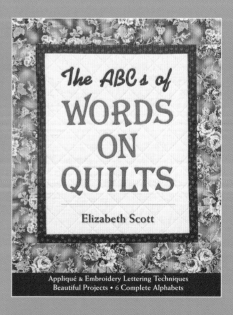